THEURGY
THEORY & PRACTICE

"P. D. Newman's *Theurgy: Theory and Practice* is a wonderfully informed book on practical theurgy, with special emphasis on its relation to what is generally referred to as 'shamanism.' The text is well-referenced, making it useful for scholars, as well as very readable, making it of value to the lay reader and practitioner. *Theurgy* is a wonderful addition to anyone's library, as there is ample material here for literally everyone."

MARK STAVISH, DIRECTOR OF STUDIES AT THE
INSTITUTE FOR HERMETIC STUDIES AND
AUTHOR OF *EGREGORES: THE OCCULT ENTITIES THAT
WATCH OVER HUMAN DESTINY*

"Theurgy is commonly thought of as a spiritual practice that began with Julian the Chaldæan in the second century CE and blended Eastern practices with rational Greek thought, primarily Neoplatonism. However, Neoplatonists such as Porphyry and Proclus pointed to theurgic elements in the archaic Homeric epics. While Eastern influences are not disputed, the author convincingly argues that they are a mere sprinkling and that the roots of theurgy are predominantly Greek, having begun at the time of Homer and practiced continuously thereafter. Readers thirsty for more knowledge about the path of theurgy will not be disappointed."

TONY MIERZWICKI, AUTHOR OF *HELLENISMOS*

"P. D. Newman tells a compelling story of the origins and development of theurgy, a fundamental spiritual practice in ancient Mediterranean religion. His argument is supported by the best contemporary scholarship on theurgy and on classical religion and philosophy. Newman has also assembled and organized a wealth of source material (in translation), which would otherwise be difficult to collect. Read this book for a fascinating exploration of theurgy over more than a millennium, from Homer to Proclus."

BRUCE J. MACLENNAN, PH.D.,
AUTHOR OF *THE WISDOM OF HYPATIA*

"A must for those interested in ancient Greek thought about souls and soul flight. According to Newman, theurgy can be traced as early as Porphyry's and Proclus's para-Homeric sources that describe *iatromanteia*, which translates to 'healer-seer' who took soul flights. Tying these types of experiences to early shamanic themes reflected in works such as the *Odyssey*, the author weaves a compelling narrative of the early history and practical importance of theurgy. Newman's analyses are thought-provoking and demand attention as he outlines a good case for how souls and the shamanic craft have shifted in antiquity from the early writings of authors such as Parmenides and Empedocles to the later Neoplatonists. The ideas contained in this book are sure to form a new starting point for many future analyses on how shamanic themes developed among the Greeks."

CHRISTINE S. VANPOOL, PH.D., COAUTHOR OF
AN ANTHROPOLOGICAL STUDY OF SPIRITS

"P. D. Newman's impressive book on theurgy and Homer covers the interpretation of myth and ritual theurgy by the Neoplatonists. With references to the Pre-Socratics, Pythagoras, Plato, and even Egyptian and Mesopotamian texts, Newman correctly understands theurgy to be distinguished from other forms of magic as initiatory and anagogic. He presents detailed and critical accounts of ancient astrological and cosmological phenomena and follows the best scholarship in developing his rather original conclusion: that Proclus and company were indeed justified in seeing in Homer the esoteric meanings they teased out of his texts. The work reveals a new angle and a new dimension of the still emerging landscape of late antique thought. It will be of interest to scholars in the field and to the general reader interested in philosophical, religious and mystical ideas."

JAY BREGMAN, PROFESSOR EMERITUS IN THE
DEPARTMENT OF HISTORY AT THE UNIVERSITY OF MAINE
AND AUTHOR OF *SYNESIUS OF CYRENE*

THEURGY
THEORY & PRACTICE

THE MYSTERIES OF THE
ASCENT TO THE DIVINE

P. D. NEWMAN

Inner Traditions
Rochester, Vermont

Inner Traditions
One Park Street
Rochester, Vermont 05767
www.InnerTraditions.com

Text stock is SFI certified

Cataloging-in-Publication Data for this title is available from the Library of Congress

ISBN 978-1-64411-836-8 (print)
ISBN 978-1-64411-837-5 (ebook)

Printed and bound in the United States by Lake Book Manufacturing, LLC
The text stock is SFI certified. The Sustainable Forestry Initiative® program
promotes sustainable forest management.

10 9 8 7 6 5 4 3 2 1

Text design and layout by K. Manseau
This book was typeset in Garamond Premier Pro with Adobe Jenson Pro and
Rosella used as display typefaces

To send correspondence to the author of this book, mail a first-class letter to the
author c/o Inner Traditions • Bear & Company, One Park Street, Rochester, VT
05767, and we will forward the communication, or contact the author directly at
pdnewman83@gmail.com.

For Algis and Zeke

For the time, efforts, and resources they've graciously invested in this little project, I am eternally grateful to the following individuals: Rebecca Newman, Susan and Mike Dye, David Brown, Alec Hawkins, Justin Ross, Jaime Lamb, Stephen Rego, Brian Alt, Ioannis Marathakis, Tamra Lucid, and Ronnie Pontiac.

The famous funeral pyre performed by Achilles for his companion, Patroclus, in Homer's Iliad *became the preliminary model for the central ritual practiced by the Theurgists—known as the "Rite of Elevation."*

Detail from 1884 engraving of Achilles sacrificing a Trojan youth, as narrated by Homer in the *Iliad* 23.181–2. Greek Apulian red-figure volute krater, attributed to the Darius Painter, ca. 330 BCE, Naples Arch Museum. The original version of this image is a black-and-white line drawing from the title page of W. H. Roscher, *Ausführliches Lexikon der Griechischen und Römischen Mythologie*, vol. 3 N–P (Leipzig, Germany: Druck und Verlag Von B. G. Teubner, 1890–1897).

CONTENTS

PART II
The Odyssey and the Iliad

FOREWORD

The emergence of theurgy in the Roman era has been a subject of much discussion. In the past it was more or less seen as an adulteration of the rational Greek thought with superstitious beliefs and practices of the East. And indeed, a superficial look at the subject may seem to corroborate such claims, since the very origin of *theurgy,* as this term was understood in late antiquity, is closely related to the eastern regions of the Roman Empire. Theurgy was ultimately based on the *Chaldæan Oracles,* a collection of obscure verses that were said to be supernaturally transmitted to Julian the Chaldæan during the second half of the second century CE.

But these *Oracles,* albeit named Chaldæan, are not written in Koine, which any denizen of the eastern parts of the empire could write, but in Homeric Greek, an extremely archaic literary dialect that suggests a serious delving into the Greek culture. The same can be said about the meter of the *Oracles.* They are written in dactylic hexameter, a rhythmic scheme of poetry that is used, among other works, in the *Iliad* and the *Odyssey,* and one would imagine that using meter while writing in this dialect would by no means be an easy feat even for an Athenian of the classical age.

Leaving aside the form of the *Chaldæan Oracles,* it can be argued that even their literary genre is characteristically Greek. Of course, most—if not all—of the ancient civilizations in the Eastern Mediterranean utilized oracles, and many recorded them, perhaps in meter as well. But the

Chaldæan Oracles are not about predictions or about making the right choice, as one would normally expect from an oracle; they are theological in nature. This feature places them among the greater corpus of the theological oracles that were issued by the sanctuaries of Apollo in Claros and Didyma, and it seems that there was no other parallel in the ancient world. As regards their content, the theology they express is Middle Platonic, and the few ritual instructions contained therein cannot be strictly attributed to Eastern cult practices, as similar rites were also taking place in Greece.

Thus, it appears that under close scrutiny, the only element that connects these religious poems to the East is solely the adjective *Chaldæan,* which probably derives from the epithet of their author. However, as nothing is known with any degree of certainty about the life of Julian the Chaldæan, this epithet could denote an ethnic Mesopotamian, a priest of a Mesopotamian deity, or even an astrologer irrespective of ethnicity; besides, his name is Latin. It is true that Neoplatonists regarded him as a Mesopotamian, but the first mention of Julian comes from the philosopher Porphyry a century later, and this information might well be wrong. But regardless of the ethnicity of the *Oracles* author, the language, meter, genre, and content of the *Chaldæan Oracles* seem to indicate that this work is more Greek than Eastern in nature.

These considerations concerning the *Oracles*, the fundamental text of theurgy, are given as an example of the problematic reasoning behind the view that theurgy is rational Greek thought adulterated with superstitious beliefs and practices of the East. This is not to say that theurgy did not take on Eastern elements in its course. There are rites vaguely described by Iamblichus in his work *On the Mysteries* that seem to refer directly to certain spells and recipes from the Greek Magical Papyri, which are more Egyptian than Greek in origin. But these elements are only secondary and serve as alternative methods of doing things; they do not change the core of theurgy. Platonists were too devoted to Plato to change the basic tenets of his doctrines. Iamblichus would not refer to Egyptian rituals for contacting one's personal daimon if the doctrine of the personal daimon had not been exposed in the *Republic,* and he would not write about the passing of the soul from the personal daimon to the ruling God if the doctrine of the twelve ruling gods had not been presented in *Phaedrus*.

It is an invalid generalization to say that Greek thought was entirely rational. There were, of course, schools of thought that focused on rationality, but this is not an excuse for such a generalization, unless one chooses to ignore the numerous references to the supernatural. The decisive step toward this realization was made in the early 1950s with the publication of the monumental work *The Greeks and the Irrational* by E. R. Dodds. It appears that it took some time for this work to be assimilated by academia, but in the last three decades, many publications and papers on the same premise have seen the light of the day.

The present book argues that the roots of theurgy can be traced as far back as Homer, that is to say as far back as the beginning of the archaic period of Greece. The first part is an overview of the ties of Greek thought with the supernatural, describing the shamanic connections of Pythagoras, Empedocles, and Parmenides that found their way into the works of Plato and were further developed by the *Chaldæan Oracles* and the Neoplatonists, thus linking the Greek shamanic practices of the late archaic period with the theurgic rites of late antiquity. The second part explores the possible relations of the *Odyssey* to theurgy, including the famous journey of Odysseus to Hades, mainly focusing on the interpretations of Porphyry in his work *On the Cave of the Nymphs,* before examining the *Iliad* in the same way, concentrating particularly on the incident of the funeral pyre of Patroclus and using Proclus's commentary on Plato's *Republic* as a guide. Finally, the book ends with a masterful analysis of the theurgic practice of animating cult statuary.

The Homeric poems are the foundational works of ancient Greek literature and formed the basis of Greek education from the classical period until late antiquity. It is not a surprise that Proclus dedicates so much of his commentary to reconcile the high esteem they enjoyed with Plato's criticism of them. Even if one is not inclined to accept an actual linear continuity between Homeric era practices and theurgy, there can be little doubt that the latter was at least influenced by the *Iliad* and the *Odyssey,* as it was formed within this particular social environment.

IOANNIS MARATHAKIS,
AUTHOR OF *THE BOOK OF WISDOM
OF APOLLONIUS OF TYANA:
APOTELESMATA APOLLONII*
ATHENS, GREECE

INTRODUCTION

The subject of this book is theurgy. Coined by the Juliani in the second century CE[1] in their work, the *Chaldæan Oracles, theourgia* is a combination of the Greek words *theos* (divinity) and *ergon* (work), meaning "to work with deity" or, perhaps, "the work of deity." Radcliffe G. Edmonds III, professor of Greek in the Classics Department at Bryn Mawr College, has distinguished between two varieties of theurgy: *telestic* and *anagogic*. "[The] former refers to the perfection or purification of mortal and material things," Edmonds writes in his book *Drawing Down the Moon: Magic in the Greco-Roman World,* "while the latter is a 'leading up' of the individual."[2] Not to be confused with *thaumaturgy* (wonder-working), *magia* (magic),* or *goetia* (the evocation of demons), although the practice shares similarities, theurgy essentially concerns the reorientation—and eventual union—of the individual soul with the divine Monad or One.† Theurgy may therefore be seen as a system both philosophical and technical, the ultimate goal of which is the complete ontological reversion of the soul with her creator. Ergo, practically, and in Judeo-Christian terms, theurgy is effectively the Hebrew book of Genesis acted out backward—a veritable reversal of the Fall and a subsequent "reintegration,"[3] as Martinèz de Pasqually called it, of one's being into its

---

*In *De mysteriis* III.28, Iamblichus contrasts *theourgikōs* with *technikōs,* the latter of which he seems to conflate with *magia* (Iamblichus, *On the Mysteries,* 189–91).
†The One in Neoplatonism refers to the highest good, equated with Aristotle's *Unmoved Mover.*

pēgē or source. The endgame of theurgy—*henosis* (mystical union)—is thus the same as that of *hesychasm* in the Eastern Orthodox Christian Church, a monastic tradition in which practitioners seek divine quietness through uninterrupted prayer and contemplation of God. Both theurgy and the practice or tradition of *hesychasm* seek *theosis,* defined as union with God or the deification of humanity. Within the domain of theurgy, the means by which such an apotheosis or divinization is accomplished is via a series of anabatic or upward-moving flights through the various levels of the heavenly cosmos—an anagogic *epistrophe* or repetition through the fatal causality of the seven planetary spheres and into the region called the Ogdoad and the Ennead—the Hermetic realms of the Ogdoad and the Ennead, as the two superior Hypostases, Nous and Monad, are referred to in the ancient Hermetic treatise *The Discourse on the Eighth and the Ninth.*[4]

Outside of the Juliani, the first real mention of theurgy is by the Neoplatonic philosopher Porphyry of Tyre (ca. 234–305 CE). As historian Crystal Addey has argued, Porphyry plays the role of antagonist in his *Letter to Anebo,* setting up philosophical problems for his able successor, Iamblichus of Chalcis (245–325 CE), to neatly solve in the latter's homage to theurgy, *On the Mysteries of the Egyptians, Chaldæans, and Assyrians,* resulting in a novel and dynamic representation of two genres of philosophy: problems and solutions (a method of exegesis within Platonism) and the traditional Platonic dialogue.[5] Although, even before Porphyry was setting up questions for Iamblichus to knock down, the former had already basically set forth the theory underlying practical theurgy in sections nine through thirteen of his book *On the Cave of the Nymphs,* an allegorical commentary on Book XIII.102–12 of Homer's *Odyssey.* Still, while Porphyry and Iamblichus provided us with the general theory behind theurgy, it wouldn't be until Greek Neoplatonist philosopher Proclus Lycius (412–485 CE) published his comment on Book XXIII.192–32 of Homer's *Iliad*—namely, Essay 6 (I.152.8–153.18)—in his Platonic commentary on the *Republic* that we would get an idea of how the ritual *praktikê* (practice) of theurgy might look. Consequently, in regard to both its theory as well as its praxis, while theurgy as such goes back no further than the Juliani and the *Chaldæan Oracles* in the second century CE, it is notable that both Porphyry* and Proclus locate the precursor and prototype of theurgy within the Homeric epics.

This point is crucial, for the model of the psyche promulgated in theurgy is remarkably similar to the picture of the soul in northern shamanism. Additionally, one dominant consensus has been that, following an influx of "shamanic"† influence from the Scythian and Thracian north, the Greek conception of the psyche or soul underwent significant developments.[6] Stanley Lombardo, a former professor of classics at the University of Kansas, writes in the preface to his dual translation of the philosophical poems of Parmenides and Empedocles, for example, that:

> Men like Pythagoras, Heraclitus, Parmenides and Empedocles [. . .] resemble Siberian and American Indian shamans—that disappeared from the Greek world in the classical period [. . .]
>
> E. R. Dodds and others, following the lead of the Swiss scholar Karl Meuli, have traced the outlines of a Greek shamanistic tradition that had contact with Asiatic shamanism in Scythia, was evidenced in the eastern Aegean rim and in Crete, and crossed over to southern Italy in the sixth century B.C. with Pythagoras. Parmenides, from Elea in southern Italy, was in this line; and Empedocles, a Sicilian, was its last representative.
>
> A shaman is trained to undertake hazardous spiritual journeys in order to exercise compassion and advance in wisdom, and he often reports his experience in the form of a song, chant or poem.

---

*The problem of Porphyry's position on theurgy will be discussed in chapter 6.

†While the term *šaman* is limited to the Tungusic peoples of Siberia and northeast Asia, *shamanism,* for better or for worse, has come to denote virtually any indigenous variety of what religious historian Mircea Eliade has called the archaic "technique of religious ecstasy" (Eliade, *Shamanism: Archaic Techniques of Ecstasy,* 4). Although, as cultural historian Jeremy Naydler has pointed out, "the mystical ascent to the sky is as central to the Hermetic tradition as it is to both Egyptian and Platonic mysticism" (see Naydler, "Plato, Shamanism and Ancient Egypt"). In any case, the accepted term for the Greek manifestation of a shaman is *iatromantis,* which means "healer-seer."

Parmenides' poem closely resembles such a report, both in the details of the journey recounted in the prologue and in the substance of what the Goddess tells him, which is that the universe and our minds form a mutually committed whole. Dodds calls Empedocles' fragments "the one first-hand source from which we can still form some notion of what a Greek shaman was really like."[7]

All that Lombardo has said of the Presocratics is also applicable to the theurgists and to the Neoplatonists. In point of fact, "the theurgists," says Peter Kingsley, a scholar recognized for his groundbreaking work on Western spirituality and philosophy, "far from just falling for the 'orientalizing craze' of the late Hellenistic period, were finding their inspiration in the same regions and types of lore that had provided much of the underpinning both for Empedocles' activities and for Pythagorean concerns over half a millennium earlier."[8]

During the eighth and seventh centuries BCE, at the time of the composition of the Homeric epics, the ancient Greeks believed that the psyche was not the locus of the self and that the soul, after death, was merely a dim shade of the person who had died, not unlike an echo.[9] Moreover, these "shades" were relegated to the province of Hades, in the underworld, where they would be consigned for the duration of their spectral existence. Sometime around the seventh and sixth centuries, however, the ancient Greeks began to see the soul as something more. Following this proposed northern shamanic influence, the soul would come to be thought of instead as the very seat of one's emotional and intellectual life. Accordingly, matter or the body came to be considered as little more than an organic container or prison for an individual's psychic vitality. Succeeding death, the soul was then free to unite with *To Hen* (the One), to intercede for the living,[10] or even to reincarnate in another physical form altogether—including "a boy and a girl and a bush and a bird and a fish" and so on, as one cunning Presocratic shaman phrased it.[11] More importantly, assuming the form of carnivorous scavengers or predatory raptors, such as carrion crows (or ravens), vultures, eagles, or falcons gave the shamanic soul the potential to leave the body, basically at will, in an indigenous phenomenon known as *shamanic flight*—what today one might call *astral flight* or an *out-of-body experience*.*

Porphyry and Proclus locate the roots of theurgy in the archaic Homeric epics and insist that prototheurgic tendencies (and thus shamanic elements) were already present in ancient Greek culture, even during the eighth century and earlier—a century or more prior to Dodds's proposed influx of shamanic influence from the "Hyperborean North." This time line directly conflicts with the proposal that the picture of the soul as a volatile and mobile entity, detected among the Greeks of the seventh and sixth centuries, was imported from the Scythians and Thracians *after* the composition of the Homeric epics.

Now, to be clear, this is not to say that presence of these shamanic elements were not imported from the North. Thrace, the northern home of the legendary Orpheus, the prototypical hero of *katabasis* in Greek mythology, or descent into the underworld, has long been associated by the Greeks with Hyperborea—Hyperborea merely implying "hyper-Boreas" or "beyond Boreas," Boreas being the Greek god of the north wind. The Orphic hymn to this deity, for example, begins:

> *Boreas, wintry blast*
> *from snowy Thrace,*
> *you make the heavens tremble*[12]

Thus, in the minds of the Greeks, Thrace and Hyperborea were, for all practical purposes, virtual cognates, for the homeland of Dionysus, whose mysteries Orpheus inaugurated, was the same Hyperborean North. However, by Hyperborea, the ancients didn't just have the North in mind; rather, what they spoke of was the *extreme* North—the North *beyond* the North. We'll get more into that below. As we shall find concerning Epimenides of Crete, a seer and

---

*Other varieties of therianthropy in shamanism include transformation into canine and equine shapes.

philosopher-poet of the sixth century BCE, there were no doubt close encounters with the Scythians as well.

Another, possibly earlier solution to the problem of the presence of shamanic and thus prototheurgic tendencies within the Homeric epics—assuming they weren't present in ancient Greek culture already[13]—is to be found with the mysterious culture(s) that lay behind the murky figures of Abaris the Hyperborean and Aristaeus of Proconnesus, both of whom betray genuine shamanic ties with central and northeast Asia.

Shrouded by the deep past—going back possibly even as early as the eighth century BCE—the character of Abaris the Hyperborean is surrounded by formidable mystery. According to the penetrating research of Kingsley, Abaris:

> clearly has the makings and the markings of a shaman—one of those strange, uncontrollable healers and mystics found across the world but especially familiar in the areas around Siberia and Central Asia. [. . .] Abaris is not a Greek name at all. [This] is precisely what, in Greek, the name Abaris meant: "the Aver." As for the Avers' ancestral home, the source of their culture and their traditions and skills: it was Mongolia.[14]

Abaris was said to have been a devotee (or even avatar) of the Hyperborean Apollo. Traveling on, or perhaps *as,* a golden arrow, Abaris covered impossible distances by flying through the air—not unlike a Middle Age witch brooming her way through the air to the Sabbath. In fact, Porphyry even gave Abaris the epithet Skywalker, a name that, thanks to George Lucas's *Star Wars* franchise, has become familiar to many. Further strengthening his ties to our healer-seers, Plato, in his *Charmides,* connected Abaris the Aver to Dodds's esteemed Thracian physicians, who used *epodai* (incantations and charms)[15] in their techniques of healing both body and soul. More curious, though, is the fact that the tenth-century Byzantine encyclopedia of the ancient Mediterranean world, known simply as the *Souda,* actually identifies

Abaris as none other than the initiator and teacher of Pythagoras of Samos, the father of Western philosophy.

Another archaic shamanic figure with a reported unnaturally long life span is Aristaeus of Proconnesus, said to have been the son of Apollo and a nymph named Cyrene. Aristaeus authored a now lost travelogue in the form of a poem titled *Arimaspea,* documenting his journey back toward the Hyperborean region from which Abaris had previously arrived. However, as one might expect, his was no ordinary expedition. Accompanied by the Hyperborean Apollo, Aristaeus is said to have made the trip through the air, in the familiar form of a raven—an animal said to be sacred to Apollo. The *Souda,* for instance, claimed he had the ability to "make his soul leave and re-enter his body at will."[16] Indeed, Pliny the Elder, in his *Naturalis Historia,* even recorded having seen a statue of Aristaeus at Proconnesus that depicted his soul emerging from his mouth in the form of a raven. Like Abaris, Aristaeus is allowed an impossibly grand life span by the Greek historian Herodotus (ca. 484–425 BCE), who has the soul-journeying iatromantis suddenly emerge from a cave after some 240 years of subterranean slumber. We will encounter more cave symbolism in the course of this work.

The seventh-century philosopher-poet Epimenides of Crete, who was famous for his preoccupation with *katharsis* (purification), ritual sacrifice, and funeral reform, is said to have fallen asleep, Rip Van Winkle–style, for fifty-seven years in the Cretan Cave of Ida, sacred to Zeus. To Epimenides's surprise, when he awoke from his half-century slumber, he possessed the gift of prophecy. Diogenes Laertius (180–240 CE), biographer of the Greek philosophers, records that Epimenides made this underworld descent in the company of none other than Pythagoras of Samos, who was known for his own katabatic feats. And, according to the *Souda,* like Aristaeus of Proconnesus, Epimenides's soul could travel out of his body at will. Significantly, when he died, it was discovered that Epimenides's aged body was decorated with strange, shamanesque tattoos, not unlike the 2,500-year-old Pazyryk mummy known as the Scythian Ukok

Princess.[17] The possibility that Epimenides held ties with the shamanic Hyperborean North therefore must be taken seriously.

The sixth-century figure Hermontimus of Clazomenae—the final figure we'll explore before moving on to the Presocratics proper—is equally curious. According to Tertullian and others, Hermontimus was known to lie as though dead while his soul journeyed to faraway locations. Upon waking, he is said to have had the ability to correctly recount the events of the places to which his soul had traveled. His wife, it is claimed, revealed his location to his sworn enemies, the Cantharidae, who maliciously burned down the house wherein his still body lay—Hermontimus's freed soul in flight. Remarkably, while none of his writings have survived to the present day, Aristotle credits Hermontimus with having first posited *nous* (meaning "mind" or "thought") to be a fundamental principle of reality—a notion that is officially attributed to Anaxagoras of Clazomenae, who no doubt postdates Hermontimus. Also of interest—if all of this weren't enough—is the fact that, Laertius says, Pythagoras went so far as to claim that he was Hermontimus of Clazomenae in a past life.[18]

Throughout part one of this study, it will be discovered that though descents to the underworld seem to become less and less of a concern the closer we get to the time of Plato and especially of the Neoplatonists, the variety of shamanic soul flights we encountered in Abaris and Aristaeus persisted and appears to have ultimately been translated and expanded into what eventually would come to be called the Chaldæan art of theourgia, or theurgy. The Presocratics, we'll learn, were far more concerned with *katabasis* (retreat or descent); the theurgic Neoplatonists, on the other hand, were wholly preoccupied with *anabasis* (advance or ascent). Although we will indeed touch upon the Presocratics in the first chapter, it is primarily the anabatic flights of the theurgic Neoplatonists with which the book is concerned.

In the pages that follow, we shall identify the precise factors that led two influential Neoplatonists to locate the Homeric epics at the very heart of theurgy. In part two, we'll take a close look at Porphyry's commentary on Book XIII.102–12 of Homer's *Odyssey* (*On the Cave of the Nymphs*), which, as we have said, provides the basic theoretical framework supporting theurgic ritual. We will also investigate cases of analogous cosmic models from Porphyry's own cultural milieu. Then we shall scrutinize Proclus's commentary on Book XXIII.192–232 of Homer's *Iliad*—again, the only substantial instance of a theurgic rite coming precisely from the pen of a known practitioner, for examples of elements pertaining to the ritual practice of theurgy. Finally, in part three, we will examine the theory and praxis behind theurgic *telestikē* (initiation) in the fascinating form of *agalma* or statue animation. But before we rush directly into the subject matter of our study, a few words are first in order with regard to the epic poet Homer.

The English guitarist Robert Fripp once said of his musical group that, rather than a specific set of individuals, "King Crimson is [. . .] a way of doing things."[19] Something of the like may be said concerning Homer. While there may not have been simply one Homer, there is certainly a way of *doing* Homer, and that way is what we would call the Homeric style. This includes the use of elements such as Homeric or Epic Greek language and dactylic hexameter, in which both the *Iliad* and *Odyssey* were composed. In addition to the more famous works, numerous other texts have been attributed to Homer, the most notable of which is perhaps the *Homeric Hymns,* a collection of thirty-three paeans in the Homeric style, each praising a different deity from the ancient Greek pantheon.

Contemporaneous with the poet Hesiod, Homer is said to have been a blind, wandering bard from Chios, an island in the northern Aegean Sea, who lived sometime during the eighth century BCE. According to legend, he was the son of the god of the river Meles and an obscure river nymph called Critheïs. His father originally gave him the name Melesigenes. However, after losing his eyesight as a young man, Melesigenes came to forever be known as simply Homer, which, Pseudo-Herodotus tells us in the *Life of Homer,* means in the Cumaean vernacular "blind man."

Although his eyes had failed him, Homer was often said to have another, more subtle variety of sight. Long before Porphyry and

Proclus began applying allegorical exegesis to these epic poems, many writers already saw Homer as a great sage and spiritual authority. Herodotus, for instance, credits Homer with privileged knowledge regarding divine subjects.

> The Greeks [. . .] were ignorant, so to speak, right up until yesterday or the day before about the origins of the individual gods and whether they were all eternal and what sort of shapes they had, for it is my belief that Homer and Hesiod were four hundred years older than myself and no more. These were the ones who provided the Greeks with an account of the origins of the gods and gave the gods their names and defined their honors and skills and indicated shapes for them. The poets who are said to have lived before these men in fact, in my opinion, lived after them.[20]

The Stoics also attributed to Homer a predilection for things hidden and divine. Indicating a belief that spiritual matters were intentionally encoded into the Homeric epics by their author(s), Strabo (63 BCE–23 CE), the Greek geographer and historian, says, for example, that:

> [e]very discussion of the gods [i.e., all theology] is built upon the examination of opinions and myths. [. . .] It is not an easy thing to solve all the riddles correctly, but when the whole mass of mythically expressed material is placed before you, [. . .] then you might more easily be able to form from it an image of the truth.[21]

This is precisely the variety of thought we shall encounter later in the Neoplatonists. In regard to what specific truth(s) Homer was privy, in the above excerpt Strabo is silent, although we may be able to get some idea of what is meant from the writings of the neighboring Pythagoreans. According to this philosophical and mystical school, Homer is credited with:

having described the music of the spheres and metempsychosis, and having presented a personification of the monad in Proteus, "who contains the properties of all things just as the monad contains the combined energies of all the numbers." [Homer] is said to have held such [. . .] doctrines as the existence of a lunar paradise, and his Sirens are transformed into the benevolent Sirens of the Pythagorizing myth of Er in the Republic.[22]

Ergo, among the ancient Greeks, our epic poet has long enjoyed a privileged position as a spiritual revelator. He was even thought of as a god in the city of Alexandria, where a temple, called the Homereion, was actually erected in honor of his worship.[23] In a similar vein, occult author Stephen Skinner reports:

> The association of Homer [. . .] with magic was strengthened by his stories about the sorceress Circe in the Odyssey. It is a traditional part of Greek culture to claim that its poetry was more than just manmade, so that quoting Homer for magical reasons for the ancient Greeks, was rather like Christians or Jews quoting passages from the Bible.[24]

In fact, Homer has been so associated with magic that sixteenth-century occult author Heinrich Cornelius Agrippa von Nettesheim went so far as to refer to the eleventh book of the *Odyssey* as "the *Necromancy* of Homer." In a similar vein, the sixteenth-century grimoire *Arbatel de Magia Veterum* credits Homer's special knowledge of *psychagogia* (i.e., necromancy) to "necromantic spirits."[25]

"Aside from their religious significance," Skinner writes, "passages from Homer were used in divination." One example of this latter case of bibliomancy is a method involving three dice, referred to as *Homeromanteion** found in the Greek Magical Papyri or *Papyri Graecae*

---

*The *Homeromanteion* is a divinatory text that uses a selection of Homeric verses. See the appendix.

Magicae (*PGM*).[26] Quotations from Homer further bracket the so-called Mithras Liturgy in the *PGM*—perhaps the most complete, illustrative ritual of soul *apathanatismos* (immortalization) surviving from late antiquity.

Homer has been referred to as "one of the most influential authors in the widest sense."[27] Along with Greek playwrights such as Aeschylus, Euripides, and Sophocles and Roman poets and prose writers, including Virgil, Ovid, and Apuleius, Homer would go on to influence even a number of ancient Greek philosophers, especially the three "Presocratic poets,"[28] as Tom Mackenzie has called them: Xenophanes of Colophon, Parmenides of Elea, and Empedocles of Acragas—all of whom adopt the Homeric style in their respective philosophical verses. Aristotle counted him among "those very ancient people who lived long before the present age and were the first to theologize,"[29] leading Porphyry to go so far as to refer to Homer as *ho theologos*,[30] the theologian. In short, in the words of Plato, Homer is veritably the man who "has taught Greece."[31]

PART I

Porphyry and Proclus's Para-Homeric Sources

1

KATABASIS AND THE PRESOCRATICS

A Survey of Underworld Descents in Philosophy Prior to Plato

Theurgy is a process of anabasis or magical ascent whereby practitioners, such as the Neoplatonists,* including Porphyry† and especially Iamblichus and Proclus, achieved *henosis* or mystical union with a deity, the Demiurge or the One.† However, anabasis was not always of primary importance, or even of interest, to many of the ancient Greek philosophers and poets. More than five hundred years before the Neoplatonists arrived on the scene, Presocratic poets and philosophers, including Pythagoras of Samos, Parmenides of Elea, and Empedocles of Acragas, were preoccupied instead with katabasis—a dreamy descent to the domain of the dead and to the dark goddess who rules over that realm.

---

*Radek Chlup speaks of a "western Neoplatonism" and an "eastern Neoplatonism," with Plotinus and Porphyry, who were largely influential in the Latin West, constituting the western Neoplatonism, and Iamblichus and Proclus, whose influence was felt more strongly in the Greek-speaking part of the Roman Empire, comprising eastern Neoplatonism (Chlup, *Proclus: An Introduction,* 16–18).

†Another word for this unitive phenomenon in use among the Neoplatonists was *systasis*.

For the Platonists, katabasis was understood as the descent of the soul into a body upon incarnation. Hades, additionally, was allegorized and viewed as the very world that we, as embodied beings, inhabit.[2] Socrates says to Callicles in Plato's *Gorgias,* for instance, "[perhaps] in reality we're dead. Once I even heard one of the wise men say that we are now dead and that our bodies are our tombs."[3] Again, in the *Phaedo,* Plato has Socrates say to Simmias of Thebes: "[we], who dwell in the hollows of [the earth], are unaware of this and we think we live above."[4] And, later in the same dialogue: "Those who are deemed to have lived an extremely pious life are freed and released from the regions of the earth as from a prison; they make their way up to a pure dwelling place and live on the surface of the earth."[5] Therefore, the only way to go, for Plato and his successors, was up—in an anabatic flight to the gods, the Demiurge and the One, through the various planetary spheres that separate the divine nous and Monad from the sensible world of appearances below. Theurgy was the means by which such an anabasis was accomplished. The Presocratics, conversely, leaving Mount Olympus to the gods for the most part, focused their energies instead upon katabasis, on transporting themselves to the netherworld.

The ancient Ionian Greek philosopher Pythagoras of Samos, recognized as the father of Western philosophy, is said to have descended to Hades by entering an underground cave. While Pythagoras left no writings of his own, the late Neoplatonic philosopher Algis Uždavinys explains that:

> the subterranean tomb-like chamber represents Hades for Pythagoras. Hence, Pythagoras descended into Hades, that is, the subterranean holy chamber (like the Holy of Holies, entered by the Jewish High Priest on the occasion of Yom Kippur) that he had made himself, according to Diogenes Laertius (*Vitae phil.* 2). When he came up, withered and looking like a Shaiva ascetic, he said that "he had been down to Hades and even read out his experiences [aloud to the crowd]."[6]

Pythagoras, it is said, also made another, earlier katabasis—this time with Epimenides of Crete. It is noteworthy that, in the fourth century after Christ, Aristippus of Cyrene connected Pythagoras to the god Apollo by interpreting the meaning of his name as a combination of the words *Pythia,* "of Delphi," and *agoreuo,* "to speak out." He was even called by some "the Pythian, others called him the Hyperborean Apollo. Others considered him Paeon," the latter being a "form of Apollo as the physician of the Gods."[7] A certain "Samian poet" even sang of the philosopher that he was actually descended from the Delphic deity.

> *Pythias, the fairest of the Samian race*
> *From the embraces of the god Apollo*
> *Bore Pythagoras, the friend of Zeus.*[8]

While Iamblichus admits doubting the above claims, he does say that "no one will deny that the soul of Pythagoras was sent to mankind from Apollo's domain."[9] In any event, when he performed his sacrifices at Delos, Pythagoras is said to have done so "at the bloodless altar of Father Apollo."[10] Iamblichus also calls him a theurgist. As an aside, one curious tidbit about Pythagoras of Samos, to which we'll return later, is that, according to Aristotle and others, the father of Western philosophy quite literally had a thigh made of gold.

Parmenides of Elea—a similarly famous, yet obscure Presocratic philosopher celebrated as both the father of logic and the father of metaphysics—wrote a dactylic hexametrical poem recounting his trip to Hades and the underworld goddess whom he encountered. After passing through the gates of Hades, at the junction of three roads, the infernal goddess instructed Parmenides as to the true nature of reality. His preom or preface to *Peri Physeôs* (*On Nature*) begins:

> *The mares that carry me as far as longing can reach*
> *rode on, once they had come and fetched me onto the*
> *legendary road of the divinity, the road that carries the*
> *man who knows through the vast and dark unknown.*

[. . .]
And the goddess welcomed me kindly and took
my right hand in hers and spoke these words as she
addressed me.[11]

As recounted in the preface, the divinity proceeds to instruct Parmenides in the laws of logic that we know today. That is, it was a mysterious, underworld goddess from whom Parmenides received the very rules of reason, with which he returned to the land of the living for the inauguration of a new era. To a world that turned on *mythos,* mythology, Parmenides introduced the novel pivot of *logos,* logic—although we must admit that the weird way in which the father of logic acquired that understanding appears to contradict the very laws with which he was entrusted.

Fascinatingly, Parmenides may have had something more in common with Homer than just simply meter. David Gallop, professor of philosophy at Trent University, notes the following in a comment to his translation of the Parmenides fragments:

> In the ninth book of the Odyssey, the Cyclops, Polyphemus, is tricked by being told that Odysseus' name is "No-one." Parmenides' familiarity with this memorable incident can hardly be doubted, and his own treatment of the word 'nothing' may even be a conscious echo of it, in keeping with the Odyssean character of his poem. [Jackson P. Hershbell] has seen the Polyphemus incident as "a dramatic illustration of Parmenidean philosophy."[12]

Although, Gallop takes issue with the interpretation of Hershbell, professor of classics at the University of Minnesota, stating that "[stupid] though Polyphemus is, he does not suppose that no one can recognize or attend to 'that which is not,'" the specific ontological dilemma to which Gallop objects here is beyond the limited scope of our study.*

---

*For a scholarly investigation into the problem of Parmenidean being, see Palmer, *Parmenides and Presocratic Philosophy.*

Comparing the Eleatic* philosopher's poem to his central and northeast Asian counterparts, Alexander P. D. Mourelatos, renowned specialist in the Presocratics and ancient philosophy, noted that, like Parmenides,

> [the] shaman is a mediator between men and god. He has the capacity of leaving his body in a trance to travel to Heaven or to the Underworld. He does this to accompany other souls, or to receive medical or cult information from a deity. His journey is a hazardous one, and calls for the protective escort of demonic powers. There may be wandering before or after the desired confrontation with the deity. The means of conveyance are sometimes flying chariots. There is certain affinity between the shaman and certain animals, especially the horse. The shaman is also often poet and singer and typically narrates his transcendental journey and experience in the first person.[13]

Like Pythagoras, Aristaeus, and Abaris before him, Parmenides was also a devotee of the god Apollo.[14]

Another who wrote in dactylic hexameter was the Sicilian poet and philosopher Empedocles of Acragas, whom Aristotle called the father of rhetoric. Except for a reference to bringing "back from Hades the strength of a man who has died,"[15] Empedocles never wrote about an actual katabasis to Hades in any of his surviving fragments. However, he himself was indeed surrounded by tales and legends closely connected to both imagery and motifs directly associated with the ancient Greek underworld—and with one of its most terrifying goddesses in particular: Hecate, whose careful control over liminal spaces included "opening and shutting the gates of Hades."[16] Hecate is generally known in the classical world as the psychopomp who escorted Persephone in and out of Hades.[17]

---

*The Eleatics were Presocratic philosophers centered in Eleas, an Italian Greek colony in southern Italy; they included—along with Parmenides—Zeno, Melissus, Xenophanes, and Empedocles.

Michael A. Rinella, in his fabulous study *Pharmakon: Plato, Drug Culture, and Identity in Ancient Athens,* introduces us to the enigmatic Empedocles.

> Empedocles combined weather magic and medical skills in a shamanic manner writing, in one surviving fragment, "you will learn pharmaka for ailments and for help against old age. [. . .] You will check the force of tireless winds, which seep over the land destroying fields with their blasts [. . .] you will bring back restorative breezes [. . .] you will bring out of Hades the life-force of a dead man." Empedocles introduces himself in his *Purifications* (115.3) as "a seer and a healer" and describes himself as "banished from the gods and wandering about."[18]

"A *pharmakon* is something that produces an effect without a visible cause," Edmonds explains: "[It] may be a material substance—a poison, a drug, a medicine, or a potion—but it may also refer to an immaterial incantation or curse."[19] Derek Collins, an associate professor of Greek and Latin at the University of Michigan, tells us that *pharmakeia* and related terms such as *phármakon* and the verb *phármakeuein* "are regularly used in Hippocratic vocabulary specifically to refer to purgatives and purgation. [. . .] The Hippocratic term for 'purification' is *katharsis*."[20] Appropriately, katharsis or purification, after which Empedocles's poem happens to be named, refers to the first stage of initiation into the ancient mysteries.

Carl A. P. Ruck, a professor in the Classical Studies Department at Boston University, has the following to say of our iatromantis or healer-seer:

> Empedocles [. . .] a shamanic healer, a *iatros* and *goes,* was said to have purified his body with "living flame" and to have "drunk fire from immortal mixing bowls or kraters." Or as another poet put it, "He leapt into a bowl of fire and drank Life." There was a tradition interpreting this as meaning that he jumped alive into

the fiery cauldron of Mount Aetna to declare his immortality, but since there is some confusion about how he died (by drowning, hanging, etc.), and his tomb was actually shown at the town of Megara, the "drink of fiery mix" no doubt refers to an entheogenic rite of ecstatic death.* Volcanoes were seen as a Cosmic axis; and in the case of Empedocles' immolation, the krater threw back up a single bronze slipper, such as the ones he was said to wear in his function as Delphic priest. The krater as chalice is not only the source of the initiate's drink, but in his experience he throws himself into its burning cauldron to achieve immortality.[21]

Góēs is another name for a sorcerer or magician and is connected to the word *goetia,* which itself is related to the practice of daimonic magic.[22] See, for example, the seventeenth-century grimoire *Lemegeton Clavicula Salomonis,* which includes the books *Ars Goetia* and *Ars Theurgia-Goetia.* The word *góēs* literally means "howler," referring in one sense to the technique of the *kletor* or theurgic caller—that is, the one doing the invoking in the ritual. Later, we shall encounter another *góēs* and *pharmakeus,* the latter meaning both "one who prepares or uses magical remedies" and "sorcerer," in the daimonic figure of Eros in our chapter on Plato's allegories and myths.

Being a *góēs,* Empedocles's poem actually fits firmly within the family of *agōgē* spells from the *katadesmoi* or curse tablets of the ancient world. As we pointed out above, Empedocles's poem refers to the *góēs* bringing "back from Hades the strength of a man who has died."[23] This, by definition, is *psychagogia,* a form of necromancy practiced by the ancient Greek *góēs.* The word *áxeis* (ἄξεις), which Empedocles uses here for "bring back," is in fact a conjugation of *agō,* "to fetch," which forms the root of *agōgē.* Interestingly, looking back at Parmenides, right there in line two he uses the form *agousai.* What is interesting here is that Parmenides uses the phrase to refer not to his leading of a person

---

*The Greek word *pharmakeia* is usually translated as "sorcery," but it can also mean "entheogenic or psychedelic plants"; the word is etymologically connected to both remedies and poisons.

or soul, but rather in reference to his being led into Hades by the "mares that carry [him] as far as longing can reach."

Empedocles was also an accomplished musician. For instance, Iamblichus records the following fascinating account, which has the man from Acragas employ Homeric verse in the form of what Christopher Faraone, professor of classics at the University of Chicago, has called "hexametrical *pharmaka*."²⁴

> Once, a certain man drew a sword on Empedocles' host, Anchitus. [. . .] Empedocles, since he had the lyre, changed its tuning, played a softening and soothing strain, and immediately struck up the line, "free from sorrow and lacking anger, forgetful of all ills" [Od. 4.221], in the words of the poet, he saved his own host, Anchitus, from death, and the young man from homicide. And it is reported that this man then became the most distinguished of Empedocles' pupils.²⁵

Kingsley demonstrates in his remarkable book *Ancient Philosophy, Mystery, and Magic: Empedocles and Pythagorean Tradition* that a number of legends surround the mysterious death of Empedocles. The Greek philosopher Heraclides Ponticus (387–312 BCE), for instance, tells us that Empedocles didn't die but was actually taken up by the gods, not unlike the way in which the biblical prophets Enoch and Elijah were taken up by the Jewish deity prior to their transformation into the archangels Metatron and Sandalphon, respectively. According to Heraclides, Empedocles, the father of the theory of the four elements,* was *divinized,* like his Hebraic counterparts. Diogenes Laertius, on the other hand, has Empedocles impressively immolate himself in the raging fires of Mount Etna's crater, a stratovolcano on the east coast of Sicily—again, so that his followers might believe that he was subsequently transformed into a god. The English word *crater* derives from

---

*We will encounter Empedocles's elements or "roots," as he called them, later in chapter 2 in our discussion of Plato's *Timaeus.*

the Greek *krater,* which means "mixing bowl." The Roman lyric poet Quintus Horatius Flaccus (65–8 BCE), conversely, offers instead that Empedocles's self-immolation was designed to prove to his followers that he already was divine. For, in the time of Empedocles, Etna was worshipped as the veritable entrance to the Greek underworld, leading one directly not only to the domain of the dead, but also to the terrifying goddess who ruled that realm. Ergo, offerings were regularly made by Sicilian devotees of the goddess by throwing sacrifices directly into the mouth of the volcano.

After Empedocles had hurled himself into the massive crater or krater, Etna thereupon immediately erupted, spewing forth from its gaping mouth a significant, symbolic artifact: a single metallic sandal, curiously cast completely in bronze. Both these seemingly random objects—the krater and the single, bronze sandal—are in fact symbols that are very closely intertwined.

To begin with, as noted earlier, the term *krater* was an early Greek term for a mixing bowl that was used to blend wine with water and other ingredients, which was then distributed to smaller drinking cups or bowls.* This is especially true in regard to the *symposion* or drinking parties, for example, where mixed wine was ceremonially imbibed by men of all ages in a jovial atmosphere. Xenophanes of Colophon, who adopted Homer's dactylic hexametrical style, said, for instance:

> For now the floor is clean, as are the hands of all
> and the cups; [. . .] and the mixing bowl stands full of cheer.
> Another kind of wine is ready, promising it will never run out,
> a mild vintage smelling of flower in the jars.[26]

The use of the word *flower* in this context refers to the mixed wine's inebriating quality. For "a wine deficient in flower showed its lack in the nature of the resultant inebriation," explains Ruck. Moreover, "[wine]

---

*The smaller drinking cups or bowls include *skyphoi* (a *skyphos* is technically a drinking bowl), *kalyces,* and *kantharoi.*

was a generic term," and the word could just as well denote a "'strong inebriating water,' which could mean an herbal potion." "In Greek," the professor elucidates, "every drink that induced drunkenness was termed simply a wine."[27] According to Ruck:

> the Greeks did not know the art of distillation and hence the alcoholic content of their wines could not have exceeded about fourteen per cent, at which concentration the alcohol from natural fermentation becomes fatal to the fungus that produced it, thereby terminating the process. Simple evaporation without distillation could not increase the alcoholic content since alcohol, which has a lower boiling point than water, will merely escape to the air, leaving the final product weaker instead of more concentrated. Alcohol in fact was never isolated as the toxin in wine and there is no word for it in ancient Greek. Hence the dilution of wine, usually with at least three parts of water, could be expected to produce a drink of slight inebriating properties.
>
> That, however, was not the case. The word for drunkenness in Greek designates a state of raving madness. We hear of some wines so strong that they could be diluted with twenty parts of water and that required at least eight parts water to be drunk safely, for, according to report, the drinking of certain wines straight actually caused permanent brain damage and in some cases even death. Just three small cups of diluted wine were enough in fact to bring the drinker to the threshold of madness. Obviously the alcohol could not have been the cause of these extreme reactions. We can also document the fact that different wines were capable of inducing different physical symptoms, ranging from slumber to insomnia and hallucinations.
>
> The solution to this apparent contradiction is simply that ancient wine, like the wine of most early peoples, did not contain alcohol as its sole inebriant but was ordinarily a variable infusion of herbal toxins in a vinous liquid. Unguents, spices, and herbs, all with recognized psychotropic properties, could be added to the wine at the ceremony of its dilution with water. A description of such a ceremony occurs in Homer's *Odyssey*, where Helen prepares a special wine by

adding the euphoric nepenthes to the wine that she serves her husband and his guest. The fact is that the Greeks had devised a spectrum of ingredients for their drinks, each with its own properties.[28]

Conversely, as we'll see in chapter 7, the mixing bowl could also play a role in certain funeral rites and, more specifically, in rites of psychagogia. An important, early usage in this saturnal context appears in Book XXIII of Homer's *Iliad*. Perhaps one of the most poignant moments in Homer is the sacred ritual that Achilles performs for his dearly departed comrade. It is a sensitive and subtle rite, the intention of which is to safeguard the soul of Patroclus in its passage to the divine, celestial empyrean or heaven. According to Proclus, in this rich, emotional scene, Homer describes the essential spiritualizing ceremony of epic Greece.

Following a dream visitation from his deceased partner, Achilles erected a funeral pyre and performed for Patroclus a rite that Proclus explicated as the prototypical rite for theurgic elevation.[29] Homer's hexametrical hymn reads:

> *nightlong swift-footed Achilles from a golden mixing bowl, with a two-handled goblet in his hand, drew the wine and poured it on the ground and drenched the ground with it, and called upon the soul of unhappy Patroklos.*[30]

According to Syrianus, Proclus's mysterious teacher, Achilles's rituals have a symbolic meaning:

> And the tradition is that he poured out libations all night over the pyre, "from a golden mixing-bowl, drawing the double cup, invoking the soul of unfortunate Patroclus," the poet all but proclaiming openly to us that Achilles' practice concerned his friend's soul, [. . .] and that he employed everything symbolically, the golden mixing-bowl for the souls' spring and the libation for the emanation springing from it.[31]

Besides the Homeric text itself, the inspiration for Syrianus's and Proclus's association of Achilles's funerary libations with the idea of "soul" is no doubt twofold. The first influence is assuredly from Plato—whom we'll visit more closely in chapter 2—who wrote in his dialogue *Timaeus* of a divine krater wherein the Demiurge mixed psyche, or soul, for the purpose of animating the cosmos.

> [T]he Demiurge turned again to the mixing bowl he had used before, the one in which he had blended and mixed the soul of the universe. [. . .] And when he had compounded it all, he divided the mixture into a number of souls.[32]

In the same manner that Achilles "dipped wine from a golden bowl and poured it down on the ground," Plato's Demiurge "divided the mixture into a number of souls." The krater is therefore understood to be the province of the *anima mundi* or world soul, referred to by Proclus as the "spring of souls." The individual cup ladled out by Achilles alludes to Patroclus's own, individual share of soul—the same being theurgically called forth by the very symbolic act of the ritual itself.

Syrianus's and Proclus's second influence for their association of Achilles's funerary libations with the idea of soul is found in the *Chaldæan Oracles,* written by the Juliani in the second century CE, where Hecate, the goddess of the forked path,* is possessed of a mixing bowl–like "hollow." Fragments 50 to 52 read:

---

*The forked path is one of the most well-known symbols associated with Hecate. In addition to being a goddess of the crossroads (*PGM* IV.2943–66), for instance, d'Este and Rankine tell us in their lovely book *Hekate: Liminal Rites* that she was primarily a goddess of three-way streets: "[Hekate] was also *Trioditis* ('*of the three-ways*' or '*of the crossroads*'), a title which was also Latinized to *Trivia* (as *Trimorphos* was Latinized to *Triformis*). In this role she was the dreadful queen of the dead, attending the crossroads with her ghosts and *daimones*. In the Roman period when she was synchretised with Diana, that goddess also used the title and was called Diana *Trivia*. Another title connected with this role was *Enodia* ('*of the wayside*' or '*of the crossroads*'), which was originally the name of a Thessalian goddess who became assimilated into Hekate. This title was shared with Artemis, Selene and Persephone" (d'Este and Rankine, *Hekate: Liminal Rites*, 60).

50. [The] center of Hecate is borne in the midst of the Fathers.

51. Around the hollow of her right flank a great stream of the primordially-generated Soul gushes forth in abundance, totally ensouling light, fire, ether, worlds.

52. In the left flank of Hecate exists the source of virtue, which remains entirely within and does not give up its virginity.[33]

In the *Chaldæan Oracles,* Hecate is not only associated with the mixing bowl, fragment 51 imparts, in striking imagery, that this krater and Hecate are in fact consubstantial. Empedocles's self-immolation in the krater of Etna was nothing short of a complete dissolution—a *henosis*—with Hecate herself. Pythagoras of Samos, it is said, once sacrificed a *heca*tomb—a great public sacrifice of a hundred oxen. On the other hand, Empedocles, it seems, sacrificed himself to *Heca*te.

The krater also plays a role in both the *Corpus Hermeticum,* which we will encounter in more detail in chapter 5, and in the alchemical writings of the Hellenistic Gnostic, Zosimos of Panopolis. In the former, we find in a tract aptly titled "The Mixing Bowl or the Monad" that Hecate's krater of psyche has been replaced by a mixing bowl of nous or mind, which is set up amid the souls as though it were a "prize."

> He filled a great mixing bowl with [mind] and sent it below, appointing a herald whom he commanded to make the following proclamation to human hearts: "Immerse yourself in the mixing bowl if your heart has the strength, if it believes you will rise up again to the one who sent the mixing bowl below, it recognizes the purpose of your coming to be."[34]

Rather than serving to distribute soul or mind to creation in *the mixing bowl or the Monad,* the worshippers are encouraged instead to immerse themselves in the contents of the krater. This Hermetic baptismal imagery in fact recurs in another famous Hellenistic text, *The Visions of Zosimos,* where our krater is further associated with an act of katharsis, which traditionally preceded *telete* (meaning "perfection" or "initiation") in the corresponding ancient mystery rites.

I fell into a trance and saw before me a sacrificial hierophant perched atop a broad, bowl-shaped altar. [. . .] The hierophant arose and a voice from above addressed me: "[. . .] The one who sacrifices me also revives me through casting aside the heavy sediment of the body. And since by the will of necessity I am an initiated hierophant, I become spirit."

[. . .]

And I saw the same altar in the form of a bowl and at the top the water bubbling, and many people in it endlessly. And there was no one outside the altar whom I could ask. [. . .] I marveled at the boiling of the water and the men, burning yet living. [. . .] 'It is the place of the exercise called preserving (embalming). For those men who wish to obtain virtue come hither and become spirits, fleeing from the body.[35]

"Becoming spirits, fleeing from the body," Zosimos here comes quite close to the concerns of the theurgists.

Finally, Crater is the name of a small constellation found between the zodiacal signs of Virgo and Libra, right next to its sister constellations, Hydra and Corvus—the latter being significantly Apollo's pet raven. As with most constellations, there is a back story that explains the close proximity of these three in which Apollo plays a central role.[36] Commanding Corvus to take his cup (krater) and go forth to fetch him some water, the raven made the fateful decision to stop at a fig tree and await the ripening of its many fruits, which, to his corvid sensibilities, seemed nigh. After gorging himself on succulent produce, Corvus realized that much time had passed and, taking the cup in his small claws, flew to the water source and filled the cup. Almost as soon as he had filled it, however, the bird noticed Hydra, a water snake, winding her way just below the surface of the water. Holding the cup in one foot, Corvus used the talons of his free foot to snatch Hydra from her element and fly away with her to the Apollonian temple. "What took so long," the god asked his pet, already knowing full well the answer. "Truly," said the raven, "I left for the water source in swift time, but upon arriving I met a water snake that would not allow me to fill your cup, Bright Phoebus. I have therefore brought her to you so that you may take your revenge." Seeing through the bird's deception, Apollo cursed him for his lies before flinging Corvus, Hydra, and the krater far into the heavens. Corvus and the krater (later designated as Crater the constellation) were commanded to forever ride through the skies on the back of the framed Hydra—the latter being instructed to keep the disobedient bird and the krater perpetually apart, one resting near the middle of the snake and the other, near the tail. We will examine this Crater constellation more closely in chapter 6.

The single, bronze sandal, strange as it is remarkable, is tied to the foot of none other than our chthonic goddess Hecate, whom Porphyry referred to as the "goddess of the brazen sandals."[37] In the *Papyri Graecae Magicae,* for example, there are at least two spells that are of special interest to us. In the spell *PGM LXX.4–25,* titled a "Charm of Hekate Erischigal against fear of punishment," is the following:

> [T]ake hold of your right heel and recite the following: "Erischigal, virgin, bitch, / serpent, wreath, key, herald's wand, golden sandal of the Lady of Tartaros." [. . .] I have been initiated, and I went down into the [underground] chamber of the Dactyls, and I saw/the other things down below, virgin, bitch, and all the rest.[38]

Hans Dieter Betz, an American scholar of the New Testament and early Christianity at the University of Chicago, identified the above as "Fragments from a Catabasis Ritual."[39] In this rite, Hecate has been curiously conflated with the ancient Mesopotamian underworld goddess Erischigal or Ereshkigal, on whose golden throne Ereshkigal's sister, Inanna-Ishtar, had set her wanting eye when the latter made her prototypical katabasis to Kur—the Mesopotamian underworld. It is also notable that the sandal, the "Charm of Hecate," is described as being gilded or golden, as opposed to the more familiar bronze footwear that was produced following Empedocles's own brazen descent.* But, even so, in an earlier fragment (*PGM* IV.2241–358), we find an almost identical invocation of Hecate as the "waning moon." In this spell, the sandal is clearly described as being bronze—and notably, it still appears in the singular.

> *Bronze sandal of her / who rules Tartaros,*
> *Her fillet, Key, wand, iron wheel, black dog,*
> *Her thrice-locked door, her burning hearth, her*
> *   shadow,*
> *Depth, fire, the governess of Tartaros.*[40]

The association of Empedocles with Hecate is thus reinforced, and his ties with Hades are further cemented. As an aside, it is in connection with this same underworld context that the author of *Empedocles and Pythagorean Tradition* mentions Aristotle's bizarre claim that Pythagoras of Samos's right thigh—or perhaps the *hollow* of his *right flank*—was quite literally made of gold. Each of these accidents, therefore, appear to mask one and the same substance. That is, they appear to be types of the same *arche* or origin.

As another fascinating aside, Hecate plays a rather strange role in the Homeric tradition. Sarah Iles Johnston, professor of religion and academic researcher, recounts an interesting bit of lore regarding Iphigenia, the sacrificed daughter of King Agamemnon in Homer's *Iliad*. The king deeply offended Artemis, the goddess of chastity, hunting, and the moon, either by boasting he was a better hunter than her or by killing a deer in one of her sacred groves (accounts differ). To punish him, the goddess held his ships at bay with a contrary wind. Told by a seer that to make amends he must sacrifice his own virgin daughter, Agamemnon summoned her to the scene under the false pretense of marrying Achilles. However, according to the earliest attested version of Iphigenia's myth, discovered in a fragment of Stesichorus, upon being slain, the goddess Artemis caused

---

*In his *Theogony,* rather than Hecate, Hesiod describes Hera of Argos as "the one who walks in golden sandals" (Hesiod, *Theogony, Works and Days, Testimonia*, 3).

the virginal maiden to "become Hecate."[1] That is, Iphigenia was divinized and translated into the chthonic goddess herself.

The use of bronze in the context of a chthonic goddess is noteworthy as the ancient Greeks commonly associated bronze with Hades. In stark contrast to the gates of pearl and streets of gold in St. John of Patmos's vision of the New Jerusalem, the Greek road to hell was apparently paved with bronze—not with good intentions. The ancient Greek poet Hesiod, for example, wrote in regard to Tartarus that "round it runs a fence of bronze."[42] Inspired by this and perhaps by King Nebuchadnezzar II's inscription on the monumental Ishtar Gate, which reads "I fixed doors of cedar wood adorned with bronze at all the gate openings,"[43] the aforementioned lawgiver, Parmenides of Elea, penned the following words in his poem *Peri Physeôs*:

> *And with / soft seductive words the girls persuade her to*
> *push back immediately, just for them, the bar that bolts*
> *the gates. And as the doors flew open, making the bronze*
> *axels with their pegs and nails spin—now one, now the other—*
> *in their pipes, they created a gaping chasm.*[44]

We know that, for Parmenides, the choice of the phrase *bronze axels* in the above excerpt was not a haphazard one, as the poet intentionally foreshadows this line earlier in his preface when he says:

> *And the axle in the hubs let out the sound of a pipe*
> *blazing from the pressure of the two well-rounded wheels*
> *at either side.*[45]

Briefly and consequentially, these unassuming verses appear to have carried a special significance for the late Dr. Uždavinys, who cryptically said of them in connection with the "theurgic theater of the divine Eye":[46]

> Parmenides speaks about the axel of the chariot on which he rides. He mentions the "rounded wheels" (*kukloi*), or the "whirling

wheels" that can bring him to the great open threshold where the
[. . .], daughters of the Sun, hasten to the light revealed through the
Eye's rounded pupil.[47]

For Uždavinys, it seems that Parmenides's underworld descent was
understood in terms of a visionary experience.

To correct our digression, each of these apparently random
references—the krater, the single bronze sandal, and the very reference
to bronze itself—therefore, all appear to be interrelated symbols that
are closely connected with both myths of the underworld and with the
formidable goddess who is said to reside there. Thus, it stands that

> the stories of Empedocles' death weren't about his physical death at
> all. That was the crudest of misunderstandings.
>
> The legends of him throwing himself into the crater of Mount
> Etna were, in origin, coded accounts of his ritual descent into the
> world of the dead.[48]

Before moving on, it is necessary to point out that these Presocratic
katabases are not necessarily isolated incidents or even special occurrences.
In no less than some thirty-five or forty gravesites, located as far as Crete
and going all the way to Rome, many inscribed golden foils or lamellae
have been discovered. Known variously as Orphic or Bacchic golden tablets or plates, they date at least as far back as the fifth century before
the birth of Christ. These plates, oftentimes found fashioned in the
distinctive shape of an ivy leaf, were designed specifically to accompany
deceased initiates into the realm of Hades. They have been deemed by
one researcher a "source which in modern scholarship has been appealed
to more than any other single text, or group of texts, for its relevance
to Empedocles' religious ideas."[49] Possessed of often dactylic hexametrical
inscriptions that vary considerably in length—from a single, corrupted
word to as many as sixteen or more complex lines of verse—the golden
lamellae instruct disembodied souls in what to expect once they arrive on
the other side of the grave, not unlike the postmortem journey taken by

the *ba* soul though the Egyptian *dwat,* as detailed in the *Papyrus of Ani,* better known as the *Egyptian Book of the Dead* or the *Book of Coming Forth by Day*—albeit the lamellae are considerably shorter.

The longer of the tablets, Günther Zuntz, a past professor of Hellenistic Greek at the University of Manchester, divided into primarily two camps, labeled Group A and Group B. Reminiscent of Parmenides's katabatic prologue, the tablets in Group A are characterized by an underworld meeting with the goddess Nestis or Persephone, the queen of Hades, who receives the deceased "kindly" as an initiate. The plates of Group B, conversely, are marked by detailed descriptions of the topography of the underworld, replete with specific instructions on which actions one should take upon encountering certain postmortem obstacles. Their contents are admittedly both fascinating and bizarre.

In his paper "Forgetfulness in the Golden Tablets of Memory," Richard Janko, professor of classical studies, boldly attempted to reconstruct a hypothetical archetypal source text from which the golden tablets in Group B may have been derived. His execution is both laudable and educational. According to Janko, what we find in many of the Group B tablets are consistent references to two subterranean sources of water: Lēthē or Lēmosynē, the spring or river associated with forgetfulness and oblivion, and the pool of Mnēmosynē, the goddess of memory, associated with *mnēmē* or remembrance—what the Platonists called *anamnesis.* Here follows an English translation of Janko's proposed source text:

This is the (?)tablet of Memory. When he is about to die, let (the initiate) write this(?) [. . .] (lacuna) [. . .] darkness having covered (him). — (To the initiate:) You will find on the right in Hades' halls a spring, and by it stands a ghostly cypress-tree, where the dead souls descending wash away their lives. Do not even draw nigh this spring. Further on you will find chill water flowing from the pool of Memory: over this stand guardians. They will ask you with keen mind what is your quest in the gloom of (?)deadly Hades. They will ask you for what reason you have come. Tell them the whole truth straight out. Say: "I am the child of Earth and starry Heaven, but of Heaven is my birth: this you know yourselves. I am parched with thirst and perishing: give me quickly chill water flowing from the pool of Memory." Assuredly the kings of the underworld take pity on you, and will themselves give you water from the spring divine; then you, when you have drunk, traverse the holy path which other initiates and bacchants tread in glory. After that you will rule amongst the other heroes."[50]

Notably, a line reminiscent of the above—"I am the child of Earth and starry Heaven, but of Heaven is my birth"—appears in the aforementioned Mithras Liturgy from the *PGM:* "I am a star, wandering about with you, and shining forth out of / the deep."[51]

We have seen that the Presocratics—as well as the authors of the Orphic golden tablets—were almost wholly focused on incubation and feats of katabasis. But we will learn that, by the time we get to Plato and his successors, ritual descents to the underworld will be largely abandoned in favor of dialectical anabasis, *theia mania* or divine madness, and, eventually, *theourgia* or theurgy. At this point, therefore, it will be useful to make a cursory examination of the pertinent writings of Plato in search of themes that might foreshadow the theurgic motifs we'll encounter later on in the present study.

2

PLATONIC ALLEGORIES AND MYTHS

A Discussion on Plato's Reorientation of Soul Flight with Reference to His Influence on the Development of Theurgy

Confirming the esoteric nature of his dialogues, Numenius of Apamea said of Plato that:

> [h]e bound things together, yet neither in a customary nor an obvious manner. And after arranging each detail in the way he considered most suitable, and concealing himself between clarity and obscurity, he wrote in security.[1]

There are a number of ways to approach the study of the Platonic dialogues. According to the *Anonymous Prolegomena to Platonic Philosophy*, a work from the Alexandrian school's late period, the first manner is to approach them in the order that Plato himself wrote them—beginning with *Phaedrus* and ending with *Laws.* The former, the anonymous author points out, is where Plato first raises the question of whether or not he should write books. The latter, on the other hand, was left incomplete and in disarray on account of Plato's death. The second manner of approach is chronological from the perspective of the main character that figures in them, that is, Socrates. In this ordering, the list begins with *Parmenides,* when Socrates is a very young man, and ends with *Theaetetus,* which takes place after Socrates's death.

After rejecting the tetralogical model—in which it is claimed that Plato, like the tragic and comic poets, was in the habit of writing four related plays, with the fourth in the series being composed "in a humorous vein"[2]—the anonymous author proceeds to outline the ingenious approach of the Syrian Neoplatonist and theurgist Iamblichus. Following a reduction of the entire Platonic corpus to just twelve dialogues, Iamblichus arranged the books thematically and organized the remaining opus into a veritable system of Platonic initiation. This portion of the *Prolegomena* is worth repeating at length.

> The first to be explained, then, is the *Alcibiades,* because it teaches us to know ourselves, and the right course is to know oneself before knowing external things, for we can scarcely understand those other things so long as we are ignorant of ourselves. The last dialogue for discussion is the *Philebus,* because here Plato treats of the Good, which is beyond all things; therefore the dialogue, too, should come last, after all the others. Those in between should be arranged as follows. As virtues exist on five different levels, natural, ethical, social, purifying, and contemplative, we must first read the *Gorgias* because it deals with a social problem, second the *Phaedo* because it shows the way of purification, for the life of purification comes after social life. Then we come to the knowledge of reality, which is acquired through ethical (sic) virtue; this reality is observed either in thoughts or in things; after the dialogues mentioned we should therefore read, fourth, the *Cratylus,* which teaches about words, then the Theaetetus, which is about things. After these we come to

the [*Sophist* and the *Statesman*]³ which deals with natural philosophy; then to the *Phaedrus* and the *Symposium,* which are contemplative and deal with theological questions; and thus we come to the "perfect" dialogues, the *Timaeus* and the *Parmenides.*⁴

As the anonymous author of the *Prolegomena* shows, the Platonic dialogues, like the Homeric epics, occupied an important place in the teachings, beliefs, and practices of our Neoplatonic theurgists— although our concern here is less with a neat, systematic approach to the dialogues than with identifying elements within them that influenced the thoughts, actions, and writings of later theurgic practitioners. The dialogues that will be of primary interest to us here are thus few: the *Republic,* the *Timaeus,* the *Phaedrus,* and the *Symposium;* of secondary concern will be the *Phaedo* and the *Apology.* The reader doubtless noted that all of these dialogues are included in Iamblichus's reading regimen, save the *Republic.* Westerink has this to offer on the matter:

> Before Iamblichus the *Republic* seems to have been explained regularly, witness the number of authorities cited by Proclus; [. . .] Theodorus, Syrianus, and Proclus treat chosen passages. It does not follow that the *Rep.* [. . .] enjoyed less authority, for incidental quotations are extremely frequent, but they were too long to be added conveniently to the curriculum of Iamblichus (itself more than a third of the complete Plato).⁵ [Moreover, nobody] will now feel inclined, I think, to adopt [the] notion that Proclus was rash enough to discard a work on which he had written a long commentary himself.⁶

The *Republic*'s absence from Iamblichus's curriculum, therefore, should not be viewed as an indication of its lack of importance. Note that the Proclean commentary brought into question by Westerink happens to be the precise one that will occupy our interest in chapter 7 of this book and is, as we have said, the only real example of a theurgy-like rite coming directly from the pen of a known practitioner. Both Plato's original dialogue and Proclus's comment are indispensable, although Proclus did at one time famously go so far as to say that:

> [i]f I were master, the only ones of the ancient books I would have people read would be the *Chaldaean Oracles* and the *Timaeus,* and I would do away with all the others for the men of our time, because [the books] harm some of those who approach them casually and without due examination.[7]

In addition to its various discourses on the nature of the Platonic forms or ideas, the *Republic* is of interest to us at this early point in our study as the source of two important Platonic concepts, the "Allegory of the Cave" and the "Myth of Er," both of which are relevant to our investigation of Homer and theurgy. Following a lengthy discussion on personal and social justice in the *Republic,* Plato has Socrates define the tripartite soul—the rational, spirited, and appetitive parts—before moving on to deliberate on the now familiar allegory of the sun, the divided line, and the cave. In this parable, the sun represents the realm of the intelligible, while the cave signifies the realm of the sensible. On the side of the intelligible is the One or the Good; on that of the sensible, the created world of mixture and multiplicity. Betwixt these two is the divided line. Socrates's discourse in the "Allegory of the Cave" begins:

> Imagine human beings living in an underground, cavelike dwelling, with an entrance a long way up, which is both open to the light and is as wide as the cave itself. They've been there since childhood, fixed in the same place, with their necks and legs fettered, able to see only in front of them, because their bonds prevent them from turning their heads around. Light is provided by a fire burning far above and behind them. Also behind them, but on higher ground, there is a path stretching between them and the fire. Imagine that along this path a low wall has been built, like the screen in front of puppeteers above which they show their puppets. [. . .] Then also imagine that there are people along the wall, carrying all kinds of artifacts

that project above it—statues of people and other animals, made out of stone, wood, and every material. And, as you'd expect, some of the carriers are talking, and some are silent. [. . .] Do you suppose, first of all, that these prisoners see anything of themselves and one another besides the shadows that the fire casts on the wall in front of them? [. . .] What about the things being carried along the wall? Isn't the same true of them? [. . .] And if they could talk to one another, don't you think they'd suppose that the names they used applied to the things they see passing before them? [. . .] And what if their prison also had an echo from the wall facing them? Don't you think they'd believe that the shadows passing in front of them were talking whenever one of the carriers passing along the wall was doing so? [. . .] Then the prisoners would in every way believe that the truth is nothing other than the shadows of those artifacts.[8]

Such is the existential predicament Plato paints for the pitiful state of man. The world we mistake for reality is nothing more than a hall of smoke and mirrors—a mirage-like sphere of illusions, hallucinations, and fantastical fascinations—and we're chained to it. But beyond the mosaic veil of this sensible, fleeting domain lies ultimate reality—the intelligible realm of Plato's forms. Socrates compares these to the light of the sun.

Consider, then, what being released of their bonds and cured of their ignorance would naturally be like, if something like this came to pass. When one of them was freed and suddenly compelled to stand up, turn his head, walk, and look up toward the light, he'd be pained and dazzled and unable to see the things whose shadows he'd seen before. [. . .] I suppose, then, that he'd need time to get adjusted before he could see things in the world above. At first, he'd see shadows more easily, then images of men and other things [reflected] in water, then the things themselves. Of these, he'd be able to study the things in the sky and the sky itself more easily at night, looking at the light of the stars and the moon, than during the day, looking at the sun and the light of the sun. [. . .] Finally, I suppose, he'd be able to see the sun, not images of it in water or [reflected] in some alien place, and be able to study it.[9]

The goal of the theurgist is not unlike that of the prisoner in the cave—to escape the sensible world of duality and penetrate the realm of ultimate, unitive reality above. It is outside of Plato's cave and beyond his dividing line that the anagogic soul may contemplate the forms and finally unite with *To Hen,* the Monad, in what Plotinus called "mystical union with the One." As one may imagine, for the troglodyte who has contemplated the dazzling source of the light of the sun, there is no willful retreat back into the reassuring darkness of the cave, with all of its many shadows and echoes, no matter how comforting and familiar. As Socrates says:

> Instead, wouldn't he feel, with Homer, that he'd much prefer to "work the earth as a serf to another, one without possessions" [*Odyssey* XI.489–90.], and go through any sufferings, rather than share their opinions and live as they do.[10]

As we'll see in part two, a cave plays a central role in Porphyry's (and Numenius's) theurgic exegesis of Homer's *Odyssey.* Further, alongside the above considerations concerning liberation from said allegorical cave, the *Phaedo* also comes to have bearing on our current research. For in the *Phaedo,* Plato introduces the *soma-sema* equation—that is, that the *soma* or body is a *sema* or grave for the descending psyche—which we barely encountered in the introduction. A fragment from Socrates's Pythagorean contemporary, Philolaus, attested by Plato in the *Cratylus,* asserts further that "[the] ancient theologians and seers bear witness that the soul has been yoked to the body as a punishment, and buried in it as in a tomb."[11] Importantly, the cave also makes an appearance in chapter 8 of the *Corpus Hermeticum,* which we'll learn more about in chapter 5 of this book.

The "Myth of Er," another parable found in Plato's *Republic,* too is possessed of thematic ties to Homer and theurgy. This fable tells the tale of a warrior named Er who died in battle. Like Patroclus in Book XXIII of Homer's *Iliad,* Er's lifeless body is laid upon a funeral pyre. But, to his and everyone's surprise, on the twelfth day the defeated soldier rose from the dead and, similar to Hermontimus of Clazomenae and Pythagoras of Samos, proceeded to recount his experiences in the "world beyond."

> He said that, after his soul had left him, it traveled together with many others until they came to a marvelous place, where there were two adjacent openings in the earth, and opposite and above them two others in the heavens, and between them judges sat. These, having rendered their judgements, ordered the just to go upwards into the heavens through the door on the right, with signs attached to their chests, and the unjust to travel downward through the opening on the left, with signs of all their deeds on their backs. [. . .] He said that he saw souls departing after judgement through one of the openings in the heavens and one in the earth, while through the other two souls were arriving. From the door in the earth souls came up covered with dust and dirt and from the door in the heavens souls came down pure. And the souls who were arriving all the time seem to have been on long journeys, so that they gladly went to the meadow, like a crowd going to a festival, and camped there.[12]

In part two of our study, we will find that the above mentioned left and right "doors" are perhaps intentionally reminiscent of a pair of north and south "gates" appearing in Homer's *Odyssey* and with which Porphyry too will be occupied in his commentary *On the Cave of the Nymphs*. Plato's myth continues:

> Each group spent seven days in the meadow, and on the eighth day had to get up and go on a journey. On the fourth day of that journey, they came to a place where they could look down from above on a straight column of light that stretched over the whole of heaven and earth, more like a rainbow than anything else, but brighter and more

pure. After another day, they came to the light itself, and there, in the middle of the light, they saw the extremities of its bonds stretching from the heavens, for the light binds the heavens like the cables girding a trireme and holds its entire revolution together. From the extremities hangs the spindle if Necessity, by means of which all the revolutions are turned. Its stem and hook are of adamant, whereas in its whorl adamant is mixed with other kinds of material. [. . .] It was as if one big whorl had been made hollow by being thoroughly scooped out, with another smaller whorl closely fitted into it, like nested boxes, and there was a third whorl inside the second, and so on, making eight whorls altogether, lying inside one another, with their rims appearing as circles from above, while from the back they formed one continuous whorl around the stem, which was driven through the center of the eighth. [. . .] The whole spindle turned at the same speed, but, as it turned, the inner circles gently revolved in a direction opposite to that of the whole. [. . .] The spindle itself turned in the lap of Necessity And up above on each of the rims of the circles stood a Siren, who accompanied its revolution, uttering a single sound, one single note. And the concord of the eight notes produced a single harmony.[13]

Without diving too deeply into the souls and fates and lots of this portion of Plato's parable, suffice it to say that Er proceeds to describe—from the two luminaries and the five visible planets to the eighth sphere of the fixed stars beyond them—nothing shy of the entire Ogdoadic-Enneadic model of the cosmos. Plato refers to this pattern as the "Spindle of Necessity."

One line in particular from the above excerpt deserves a closer look from us:

On the fourth day of that journey, they came to a place where they could look down from above on a straight column of light that stretched over the whole of heaven and earth, more like a rainbow than anything else, but brighter and more pure. After another day, they came to the light itself, and there, in the middle of the light, they saw the extremities of its bonds stretching from the heavens, for the light binds the heavens like the cables girding a trireme and holds its entire revolution together.[14]

"In antiquity," we're informed by the brilliant independent researcher George Latura Beke, "this segment of Plato's exposition was accepted as referring to the Milky Way, with Manilius describing the Milky Way in terms that echoed Plato's words."[15] The terms in which the first-century poet and astrologer Marcus Manilius described the Milky Way are as follows:

> And just as the rainbow describes its arc through the clouds, even thus the white track marking the vault of heaven lies overhead. [. . .] Possibly the skies are coming together and the bases of two vaults meet and fasten the rims of celestial segments; out of the connection is formed a conspicuous scar making a suture of the skies.[16]

"The 'suture of the skies' of Manilius is the equivalent of Plato's 'column of light' that 'binds the heavens,'" Latura Beke adds, "and Manilius' comparison of the Milky Way to the arc of the rainbow points to Plato as Manilius' source."[17]

Before moving on, we'll reexamine one more statement at the end of Plato's above quotation: "the light binds the heavens like the cables girding a trireme and holds its entire revolution together." As the name suggests, the *trireme* was an ancient galley-style sailing vessel having three rows of oars, popular in Greece during Plato's lifetime, that played a significant role in the creation of the Athenian maritime empire. Unlike the similar *penteconter,* with its single row of twenty-five oars, and the bireme-style *diērēs,* with its pair of rows, the trireme was an enormous warship that, due to its sheer size and complexity, had to be partly held together by a set of boat cables, nearly two inches in diameter, called *hypozomata* or undergirding. The construction and application of these gigantic ropes were an official secret of Athens, and until the trireme was superseded by the larger and more efficient *quadriremes* and *quinqueremes,* their export to lands outside Athens was considered a serious capital offense. It is believed that these giant triremes were rigged from top to bottom, end to end, with the two hypozomata crossing along the middle line of the hull, just below the main beams, acting as powerful braces—"[holding] its entire revolution together." It is to these crossed hypozomata that Plato makes his curious comparison. The final image with which we are left is therefore that of the whole universe, envisaged as a great wartime ship, that is crossed about with two stellar bands, thus giving the distinct impression of the letter *X*. More will be said in regard to this Platonic character below.

In the second order of the dialogues discussed above—that is, from the perspective of Socrates—the *Republic* is immediately followed by the *Timaeus*. The *Timaeus* is an extremely important work in that Plato first develops his ideas of the Demiurge, his mixing bowl, and the anima mundi in this dialogue. Note that Demiurge simply means "craftsman" and refers to what the Masonic fraternity calls the "Great Architect of the Universe"—that is, the builder. After fashioning the universe from the four Empedoclean elements, so as to animate his creation into a living being, our Craftsman proceeded to mix the anima mundi or world soul. Significantly, he did this inside a krater, which takes us all the way back to Achilles, Xenophanes of Colophon, and Empedocles of Acragas. As we have already seen, in the *Chaldæan Oracles* the krater is connected to the figure of Hecate.

The *Timaeus* reads:

As for the world's soul, [the] components from which he made the soul and the way in which he made it were as follows: In between the *Being* that is indivisible and always changeless, and the one that is divisible and comes to be in the corporeal realm, he mixed a third, intermediate form of being, derived from the other two. Similarly, he made a mixture of the *Same,* and then one of the *Different,* in between their indivisible and their corporeal, divisible counterparts. And he took the three mixtures and mixed them together to make a uniform mixture, forcing the Different, which was hard to mix, into conformity with the Same. Now when he had mixed these two together with Being, and from the three he had made a single mixture, he redivided the whole mixture into as many parts as his task required, each part containing a mixture of the Same, the Different, and of Being.[18]

Following some further deliberation, division, and mixing of the elements of being, sameness, and difference, the Demiurge proceeded to act in a curious way that will nevertheless have bearing on our next chapter. It will also recall our aforementioned *X*.

Next, he sliced the entire compound in two along its length, joined the two halves together center to center like an X, and bent them back in a circle, attaching each half to itself end to end and to the ends of the other half at the point opposite to the one where they had been joined together. He then included them in that motion which revolves in the same place without variation, and began to make the one the outer, and the other the inner circle. And he decreed that the outer movement should be the movement of *the Same,* while the inner one should be that of the *Different.*[19]

"Plato is here describing the intersections of two celestial circles (one of the Different, the other of the Same)," Latura Beke delineates in regard to the *Timaeus,* "and he explicitly states that the movement of the Different is the circle of the Planets, the Ecliptic."[20] He continues:

Plato is not clear as to what the circle of the Same might be, just as he does not declare that his "column of light" is the Milky Way, perhaps respecting a Pythagorean injunction against revealing too much (Cicero, Iamblichus). But he does make an authoritative statement at the very end of Timaeus, that the Cosmic Soul, which he has described as having the shape of two intersecting circles (with an X at each intersection) is a "visible [. . .] perceptible god."[21]

It will be noted that, on the report of Psellus, it was in this same *X* shape that the postmortem soul of Plato is considered to have dictated to the Juliani the revelatory collection known as the *Chaldæan Oracles.* At this point in our treatment, the reader may very well be asking himself, "Are we still talking about the same Plato?" And that's understandable. To quote Earl Fontainelle, the host of the *Secret History of Western Esotericism Podcast,* in the current Platonic territory, "we are very far indeed from your Introduction to Philosophy class."[22] Hopefully, if we are successful, this will all make at least some sense by the end of the book.

At this point in the dialogue, the Craftsman took a step back from his creation and admired it in motion, praising it as "a thing that has come to be a shrine for the everlasting gods"[23]—that is, as an animated *agalma* or ensouled cult statue, for it will be shown in the final chapter that animating cult statues, a variety of *telestikē,* was a central concern for the practicing theurgists—and was in fact not unknown to our epic poet Homer.

Timaeus continues:

> The Demiurge turned again to the mixing bowl he had used before, the one in which he had blended and mixed the soul of the universe. He began to pour it into what remained of the previous ingredients and to mix them in somewhat the same way, though these were no longer invariably and constantly pure, but of a second and third grade of purity. And when he had compounded it all, he divided the mixture into a number of souls equal to the number of the stars and assigned each soul to a star. He mounted each soul in a carriage, as it were, and showed it the nature of the universe.[24]

Timaeus's mention here of a "soul carriage" is worth a second look. The reader will immediately recall from chapter 1 that Parmenides's otherworld journey took place in a mare-drawn chariot. However, Timaeus's chariot will take on major significance among the later Middle Platonists and especially the Neoplatonists, coming to be explained with reference to a pneumatic *ochēma* or "soul vehicle." Plato describes this soul vehicle as a chariot—*ochēma* being the Greek word commonly used to designate such. According to Platonic doctrine, this pneumatic ochēma not only enables the bonding of the soul to its bodily container, but it also sanctions the very phenomenon of soul flight. Edmonds explains:

> [The] immaterial soul is imagined to be carried down into the material body in a vehicle (ochēma) that is neither immaterial nor entirely material. Combining Plato's reference to the visible vehicles of the divine stars and Aristotle's designation of the stuff of stars as the fifth element of *pneuma,* later thinkers saw the vehicle of the soul as made of *pneuma,* sometimes illuminated with light like the stars and sometimes clouded and murky with the stains of lower matter.[25]

The soul chariot will become a central concern for our Athenian philosopher in a work titled the *Phaedrus.*

Alongside the *Republic,* the *Phaedrus* is one of only two of Plato's dialogues that portrays its protagonist, Socrates, as standing outside the concerns of a working society. Here, his interests are with the immortal, volatile model of the human soul. The main points that will be of interest to us in the *Phaedrus* are Socrates's lecture on the four varieties of theia mania (divine madness) and the allegory of the chariot. We shall begin with the former. "[In] fact the best things come from madness," Socrates says, "when it is given as a gift of the god."

> The prophetess of Delphi* and the priestess at Dodona are out of their minds when they perform that fine work of theirs for all of Greece, [. . .] but they accomplish little or nothing when they are in control of themselves. [. . .] The people who designated our lan-

---

*The Pythia or high priestess at Delphi is said to have relied on both ethylene gas from a nearby volcanic vent (Spiller et al., "The Delphic Oracle: A Multidisciplinary Defense of the Gaseous Vent Theory") and the incinerated seeds of the hallucinogenic *Hyoscyamus niger* or black henbane, also known as the "plant of Apollo" (U.S. Forest Service. "The Powerful Solanaceae: Henbane") in her ability to perform *mantikê* or divination.

guage in the old days never thought of madness as something to be ashamed of or worthy of blame; otherwise they would not have used the word "manic" for the finest experts of all—the ones who tell the future—thereby weaving insanity into prophecy. They thought it was wonderful when it came as a gift of the god, that's why they gave its name to prophecy; [. . .] madness (mania) from a god is finer than self-control of human origin.

Next, madness can provide relief from the greatest plagues of trouble that beset certain families because of their guilt for ancient crimes: it turns up among those who need a way out; it gives prophecies and takes refuge in prayers to the gods and in worship, discovering mystic rites and purifications that bring the man it touches through to safety for this and all time to come. So it is that the right sort of madness finds relief from present hardships for a man it has possessed.

Third comes the kind of madness that is possession by the Muses, which takes a tender virgin soul and awakens it to a Bacchic frenzy of songs and poetry that glorifies the achievements of the past and teaches them to future generations. If anyone comes to the gates of poetry and expects to become an adequate poet by acquiring expert knowledge of the subject without the Muses' madness, he will fail, and his self-controlled verses will be eclipsed by the poetry of men who have been driven out of their minds.[26]

[. . .]

We [. . .] distinguished four parts within the divine kind [of madness] and connected them to four gods. Having attributed the inspiration of the prophet to Apollo, of the mystic to Dionysus, of the poet to the Muses, and the fourth part of madness to Aphrodite and to [Eros], [. . .] the madness of [eros] is the best.[27]

Hermias, who studied Platonism under Syrianus alongside Proclus, relates Socrates's four forms of divine madness to theurgy directly. "Plato speaks about [. . .] inspiration (*enthousiasmós*)," Hermias relays from Syrianus, "which illuminates the soul with divine light."

There are different levels of inspiration, however, depending on the part of the soul that the light falls upon: it may affect the one in the soul, the soul's intellect, discursive thought or irrational parts. [. . .] Poetic madness corresponds to the lowest of these illuminations, harmonizing discordant parts of the soul. [. . .] The second place belongs to "initiatory" (*telestikē*) madness, which illuminates the soul in its proper discursive essence, thereby helping it to bring its discursivity to perfection and transcend it: "it actualizes the entire soul and makes it complete, so that even its intellective part may be active." [. . .] Prophetic madness illuminates the soul's intellect, allowing it to get beyond itself and revert upon the one in the soul. [. . .] "Finally, erotic madness takes over the soul in its unified state and connects the one in soul to the gods and to intelligible beauty."[28]

Poetic madness, Socrates says, is the province of the Muses. Telestikē madness, on the other hand, is under the rule of Dionysus. Prophetic madness, then, is associated with Apollo, and erotic madness is under the aegis of Aphrodite or Eros. Interestingly, Hermias goes on to explain, per Syrianus, that "in the sphere of external ritual activity [. . .] *telestikē* 'is ranked above all the other types of madness in that in a sense it also comprises all the others in itself—including theology, philosophy and indeed all erotics.'"[29]

Notably, like Socrates's theia mania, shamanism has usefully been described as an example of divine madness.[30] Shamans are essentially mystics. The Scottish psychiatrist R. D. Laing said famously that "[mystics] and schizophrenics find themselves in the same ocean, but the mystics can swim whereas the schizophrenics drown."[31] Shamans, then, are to psychotics what gold medalist Olympians are to nonswimmers. Indeed, we might even say that where the insane sink, shamans moonwalk—and theurgists spacewalk.

In the allegory of the chariot, which continues the imagery of the soul carriage first evoked in the *Timaeus,* Plato has Socrates liken the soul to "the natural union of a team of winged horses and their charioteer." Additionally, hearkening back to the Demiurge and his mixing bowl, Socrates adds, "[the] gods have horses and charioteers that themselves are all good and come from good stock besides, while everyone else has a mixture."

> To begin with, our driver is in charge of a pair of horses; second, one of his horses is beautiful and good and from stock of the same sort, while the other is the opposite and has the opposite sort of bloodline. This means that chariot-driving in our case is inevitably a painfully difficult business.[32]

The perceptive reader may have processed that Plato's allegory is very reminiscent of another involving a horse-drawn chariot called *ratha kalpana,* appearing in the Hindu *Katha Upanishad.* Below are verses 1.3.3–1.3.4 of Max Müller's famous translation.

> *Know that the Atman is the rider of the chariot,*
> *and the body is the chariot.*
> *Know that the Buddhi is the charioteer,*
> *and Manas is the reins.*
> *The senses are called the horses,*
> *the objects of the senses are their paths.*
> *Formed out of the union of the Atman, the senses*
>   *and the mind,*
> *him they call the "enjoyer."*[33]

But the ochēma isn't just possessed of symbolic significance. Like an *æthyric* or etheric rocket ship, this pneumatic vehicle can potentially shuttle one's soul throughout the created cosmos and back into its homeland, the "place beyond heaven." Plato describes the journey home.

> Now Zeus, the great commander in heaven, drives his winged chariot first in the procession, looking after everything and putting all things in order. Following him is an army of gods and spirits

arranged in eleven sections. Hestia is the only one who remains at the home of the gods; all the rest of the twelve are lined up in formation, each god in command of the unit to which he was assigned. [. . .] When they go to feast at the banquet they have a steep climb to the high tier at the rim of heaven; on this slope the gods' chariots move easily, since they are balanced and well under control, but the other chariots barely make it. The heaviness of the bad horse drags its charioteer toward the earth and weighs him down if he has failed to train it well, and this causes the most extreme toil and struggle that a soul will face. But when the souls we call immortal reach the top, they move outward and take their stand on the high ridge of heaven, where the circular motion carries them around as they stand as they gaze upon what is outside heaven.

The place beyond heaven—[. . .] What is within this place is without color and without shape and without solidarity, a being that really is what it is, the subject of all true knowledge, as is the mind of any soul that is concerned to take in what is appropriate to it, and so it is delighted at last to be seeing what is real and watching what is true, feeding on all this and feeling wonderful, until the circular motion brings it around to where it started. [. . .] And when the soul has seen all the things that are as they are and feasted on them, it sinks back inside heaven and goes home. On its arrival, the charioteer stables the horses by the manger, throws in ambrosia, and gives them nectar to drink besides.[34]

In practice, this anagogic ascent of the individual psyche to the "place beyond heaven" is generally outlined as a seven- or three-stage process, whether we are viewing it from the perspective of the levels as being planetary or hypostatic. In the first case, the "place beyond heaven" alludes to the Ogdoad, the region of the fixed stars, beyond the seven planetary heavens that constitute psyche; in the latter, it refers to the nous, which, while answering to the second hypostasis in Plotinus's system, is the third checkpoint when viewed from the perspective of matter—psyche being the buffer betwixt what the Peripatetics called *hyle* or matter and nous or mind in the later hypostatic system of Plotinus. Therefore, when Paul made his spontaneous ascent to the "Third Heaven," per *2 Corinthians,* for instance, it would have been in the noetic Ogdoad, loosely equated here with nous, where he most likely found himself. Socrates continues:

> Now that is the life of the gods. As for the other souls, one that fol-
> lows a god most closely, making itself most like that god, raises the
> head of its charioteer up to the place outside and is carried around
> in the circular motion with the others. Although distracted by the
> horses, the soul does have a view of Reality, just barely.[35]

This notion of only raising the head of the charioteer into ultimate reality, while his body remains inside the sensible realm, will appear again in chapter 7 with Proclus's theurgic exegesis of Homer. There, too, it is only the head of the initiate that is left exposed—the rest of his body having been totally buried. We see something similar also in the so-called Mithras Liturgy from the *Papyri Graecae Magicae,* where the one doing the ascending is solely allowed to *look* into the open doors of heaven, but not enter them.

The final point to be discussed before moving on from Plato's influential dialogues is our æthyric rocket's fuel—the very substance that sanctions said soul ascent: Eros. In Iamblichus's *paideia,* the *Symposium,* because it is "contemplative" and deals with "theological questions," immediately follows the flights of soul in the *Phaedrus.* As we saw in chapter 1 in regard to the poem of Xenophanes of Colophon, the *symposion* was a regular social event where wine (among other ingredients, often psychoactive) was ritually mixed in a ceremonial krater before being passed out to the drinkers. The setting for Plato's *Symposium* is just such an atmosphere. Socrates tells his companions of the enchanting Diotima, a priestess of the Eleusinian mysteries, who challenged him with one of the most celebrated speeches in all of Plato's many dialogues. After telling Socrates in no uncertain terms that "[Eros] is a great [daimon]" who exists "between mortal and immortal" and that "[everything daimonic] is in between god and mortal," Diotima explained to Socrates the function of these daimones.

> They are messengers that shuttle back and forth between the two, conveying prayer and sacrifice from men to gods, while to men they bring commands from the gods and gifts in return for sacrifices. Being in the middle of the two, they round out the whole and bind fast the all to all. Through them all divination passes, through them the art of priests in sacrifice and ritual, in enchantment, prophecy, and sorcery. Gods do not mix with men; they mingle and converse with us through [daimones] instead, whether we are awake or asleep. [. . .] These [daimones] are many and various, then, and one of them is [Eros].[36]

According to the Platonists, between humanity and the gods, the "great chain of being" is populated with a hierarchy of daimonic entities. The duty of these spiritual beings is to carry the aspirations of humanity up to the gods in the form of prayers, offerings, and sacrifices and to bring inspiration from the gods back down to humanity in the form of oracles, spiritual texts, and divine possessions. Here, Diotima counts Eros, one of Socrates's varieties of theia mania or divine madness as a "great [daimon]." Moreover, Socrates asserts that the "mediative daimonic eros" is a *goes kai pharmakeus kai sophists,*[37] meaning "a [clever sorcerer][38] with enchantments, [narcotic] potions, and clever pleadings."[39] Notably, Socrates himself even claims in Plato's *Apology* to be possessed of a certain daimonion whose articulations and urgings informed and regulated the condemned philosopher's behavior throughout his life. "I have a divine or spiritual [daimonion]," Socrates confesses.

> This began when I was a child. It is a voice, and whenever it speaks it turns me away from something I am about to do, but it never encourages me to do anything.[40]

Diotima begins her extraordinary oration concerning the elevating effects of daimonic Eros—Love personified—as follows:

A lover who goes about this matter correctly must begin in his youth to devote himself to beautiful bodies. First, if [Eros] leads aright, he should love one body and beget beautiful ideas there; then he should realize that the beauty of any one body is brother to the beauty of any other and that if he is to pursue beauty of form he'd be very foolish not to think that the beauty of all bodies is one and the same. When he grasps this, he must become a lover of all beautiful bodies, and he must think that this wild gaping after just one body is a small thing and despise it.

What the priestess is explaining to Socrates is that a person is only beautiful—and only possesses beauty—insofar as he participates (*methexis*) in the Platonic form of beauty. In Plato, beauty is a form. To have it is to participate in it. For the later Platonists, we shall find, the Good will be elevated all the way to the hypostatic level of the One.

After this he must think that the beauty of people's souls is more valuable than the beauty of their bodies, so that if someone is decent in his soul, even though he is scarcely blooming in his body, our lover must be content to love and care for him and to seek to give birth to such ideas as will make young men better. The result is that our lover will be forced to gaze at the beauty of activities and laws and to see that all this is akin to itself, with the result that he will think that the beauty of bodies is a thing of no importance. After customs he must move on to various kinds of knowledge. The result is that he will see the beauty of knowledge and be looking mainly not at beauty as a single example [. . .] but the lover is turned to the great sea of beauty, and, gazing upon this, he gives birth to many gloriously beautiful ideas and theories, in unstinting love of wisdom, until, having grown and been strengthened there, he catches sight of such knowledge . . .

You see, the man who has been thus far guided in matters of [Eros], who has beheld beautiful things in the right order and correctly, is coming now to the goal of Loving: all of a sudden he will

catch sight of something wonderfully beautiful in its nature; that
[. . .] is the reason for all his earlier labors:

First, it always is and neither comes to be nor passes away, neither waxes nor wanes. Second, it is not beautiful this way and ugly
that way, nor beautiful at one time and ugly at another, nor beautiful in relation to one thing and ugly in relation to another; nor is
it beautiful here but ugly there, as it would be if it were beautiful
for some people and ugly for others. Nor will the beautiful appear
to him in the guise of a face or hands or anything else that belongs
to the body. It will not appear to him as one idea or one kind of
knowledge. It is not anywhere in another thing, as in an animal, or
in earth, or in heaven, or in anything else, but itself by itself with
itself, it is always one in form; and all the other beautiful things
share in that, in such a way that when those others come to be
or pass away, this does not become the least bit smaller or greater
nor suffer any change. So when someone rises by these stages,
through loving [. . .] correctly, and begins to see this beauty, he has
almost grasped his goal. This is what it is to go aright, or be led by
another, into the mystery of Love: one goes always upwards for the
sake of this Beauty, starting out from beautiful things and using
them like rising stairs: from one body to two and from two to all
beautiful bodies, then from beautiful bodies to beautiful customs,
and from customs to learning beautiful things, and from these les-
sons he arrives in the end at this lesson, which is learning of this
very Beauty, so that in the end he comes to know just what it is to
be beautiful.

[. . .]

[How] would it be [. . .] if someone got to see the Beautiful itself,
absolute, pure, unmixed, not polluted by human flesh or colors or
any other great nonsense of mortality, but if he could see the divine
Beauty itself in its one form? [In] that life alone, when he looks at
Beauty in the only way that Beauty can be seen—only then will it
become possible for him to give birth [. . .] to true virtue (because
he is in touch with the true Beauty). The love of the gods belongs to

anyone who has given birth to true virtue and nourished it, and if any human being could become immortal, it would be he.[41]

"Using them like stairs," the theurgist may ascend through this dai-monic, hierarchical *seira* (series) that is the "great chain of being" descending from the One to the many and finally contemplate "the divine Beauty itself in its one form" in the world of the Platonic ideas. Diotima likens the daimones to eros because it is in fact love, or more specifically *philia* (friendship), that cements this spiritual, weblike structure into a coherent unity—a force the Stoics called *sympatheia*—resulting in what Iamblichus quaintly referred to as "a single system and [. . .] a single perfection."[42]

Necessarily, the above sketch barely scratches the surface of the Platonic corpus. But it should provide the reader with some notion of the ideas that would go on to find themselves operating within the minds of the theurgists. From Plato, we'll now turn to the *Chaldæan Oracles,* which John M. Dillon, an Irish classicist and philosopher, has included in what he calls the "Platonic Underworld,"[43] to continue our assessment of Porphyry's and Proclus's para-Homeric sources.

3

THE CHALDÆAN ORACLES AND THEURGY

A Discussion on the Official Emergence of Theurgy from Platonic Metaphysics

Recollect that, in the *Timaeus,* the Demiurge:

> sliced the entire [anima mundi] in two along its length, joined the two halves together center to center like an X, and bent them back in a circle, attaching each half to itself end to end and to the ends of the other half at the point opposite to the one where they had been joined together.[1]

The theurgists seem to have taken the Athenian at his word. Gregory Shaw, a professor of religious studies at Stonehill College, Massachusetts, writes in his brilliant book on the Neoplatonism of Chalcidensis that:

> Iamblichus speaks of diviners who invoke the gods with "characters" (*charaktēres*) sketched on the ground [. . .] (DM 129, 14–131).

[And] Proclus, in his commentary on the *Timaeus,* says the chi (X) (*Tim.* 36b) "was the 'character' (*charactēr*) or 'shape' (*schēma*) most evocative for recollecting the divinization of the world and our souls" (*In Tim.* II. 247, 14–29).[2]

Thus, Ilinca Tanaseanu-Döbler, a professor of religious studies at the Georg-August University of Göttingen, can say that "the two intersecting circles of 'sameness' and 'otherness' forming the X-shaped sphere are the [*character*], the ritually efficient symbol of the cosmic soul."[3] Fascinatingly, according to Ruth Majercik, professor of religious studies and classics, "it may well be that the [*Chaldæan*] *Oracles* themselves were transmitted via the theurgic technique of 'calling' and 'receiving,' with Julian the Theurgist functioning as the 'medium' through whom Julian the Chaldæan extracted oracles from Plato's soul."[4]

Hebrew linguist and historian Hans Lewy further illustrates this notion.

Julian the Chaldæan "beheld" Plato's soul and "questioned it at will." [The] philosopher's soul became visible as a geometrical luminous figure. The belief that apparition of the soul consists of semi-circles and of the character X derives from Plato's *Timaeus,* upon which Chaldæan metaphysics are based. [. . .] We may accordingly surmise that the individual souls, regarded as the offshoots of the Cosmic Soul, were represented by the Chaldæans as being, as it were, her miniature copies.[5]

While Plato's *X*-shaped soul may indeed have acted as the mouthpiece, it appears to have been speaking on the behalf of two deities that have been present with us since the beginning of this study: Socrates's god of prophetic madness, Apollo, the deity of Abaris, Aristaeus, Pythagoras, Parmenides, and the same god that declared through the Pythian, his oracle at Delphi, that no man was wiser than Socrates;[6] and Hecate, the underworld goddess who haunted us throughout chapter 1. Both of them seem to be doing the dictating in the *Oracles.* This and the dactylic hexametrical nature of the verses firmly ties the fragments to the Greek oracular *mantikê* (divination) tradition—and loosely to the Homeric style.

The Juliani—Julian the Chaldæan and Julian the Theurgist—were a father-son team of philosopher-theurgists living during the reign of Marcus Aurelius. According to the *Souda,* the father, Julian the Chaldæan, was the author of four works, now lost, on the subject of daimones. Similar to Abaris in Plato's *Charmides,* Julian the Chaldæan was also said to have constructed magical charms or healing amulets, in this case corresponding to each part of the human body. The younger Julian, on the other hand, wrote on the topics of theurgy, statue animation, and rites of initiation (telestikē) and produced oracles (like the *Chaldæan Oracles*). On the report of the later Neoplatonists, he also wrote on the subject of celestial zones. Again, according to the *Souda,* the tenth-century Byzantine encyclopedia:

> On one occasion, when the Romans were suffering from thirst, [Julian the Theurgist] suddenly created and summoned up dark-colored clouds and let loose heavy rain along with thunder and lightning bolts one after another. And this [. . .] by some cleverness Julian achieved.[7]

According to Majercik, the *Oracles* were probably received in a call-and-response format, with Julian the Theurgist in a medium-like trance and his father, the Chaldæan, doing the invoking.

Referred to by the Belgian archaeologist and historian Franz Cumont as the "Bible of the Neoplatonists,"[8] the theology articulated in the *Oracles* is decidedly Platonic, with the highest deities existing as a hypostatic triad. At the apex of this trinity is the Monad, called in the *Oracles* the First Father and the Paternal Intellect, which is wholly transcendent and is in fact described in the fragments as being "snatched away" and "existing outside" creation in a "fiery Abyss." As the Paternal Intellect, it is the function of this hypostasis to *think* the Platonic forms or ideas that will *in-form* creation below. He is also called Once Transcendent.[9]

The second hypostasis, called the Second Intellect, too is imagined as male and paternal. Although, this hypostasis, as opposed to being completely transcendent, is demiurgic. An important comparandum is the Demiurge in Plato's *Timaeus*. It is his function to fashion what the *Oracles* call the empyrean or world of intelligibles on the model of the First Father's forms. Majercik expounds:

> [T]he Second Intellect (as Demiurge) is said to project the Platonic Ideas ("divisions" or "lightning-bolts") onto primal matter (or "wombs" of the World Soul) like Zeus hurling his thunderbolts [. . .]. By this "action," the initial movement towards material creation begins.[10]

This demiurgic hypostasis is also called Twice Transcendent.

While the first two hypostases are paternalistic, the third deity in the holy trinity of the *Chaldæan Oracles* is described as feminine. Called Dynamis (Power), this figure is generally identified with the chthonic goddess Hecate, who is usually cast as the anima mundi or world soul. However, classics professor John F. Finamore, along with R. M. van den Berg and Sarah Iles Johnston, has argued that Hecate is placed too high in the Chaldæan system to be one and the same with the anima mundi.

> Power is not the Intellectual World Soul but rather an intelligible entity, we can see that the correct interpretation of fr. 6 is that this is an intelligible intermediary and separates the two Intellects. In such a position it is necessarily closer to the Father than the second Intellect is. Power is the actualized emanation from the Father, which at once helps preserve his transcendence while insuring a conduit to the world below.[11]

Indeed, as van den Berg pointed out, in the *Oracles,* Hecate is said to be the cause of soul—but not soul itself. Rather, Hecate is acknowledged as a goddess of liminality who exists in the space between two realms, such as she served when acting in the role of psychopomp for Persephone in the Eleusinian mysteries. Whereas the anima mundi in Plotinus's system acts as a buffer betwixt nous and hyle, for instance, in the *Oracles,* we find Hecate described as a "girdling membrane," separating the transcendent

First Father from the demiurgic intellect. Her right hip or flank, it will be recalled, is possessed of a krater-like "hollow" from which the goddess issues psyche.

In addition to the hypostatic triad of primary deities, there is in the *Oracles* a subpantheon of spiritual beings who play important roles in the Chaldæan theology. These are the Iynges, the Synocheis, and the Teletarchai. The reader familiar with nineteenth-century occult literature may recognize these from Aleister Crowley's *Liber XXV: The Star Ruby,* wherein, along with daimones, they replace the traditional Hebrew archangels in an updated (antiquated?) draft of the Hermetic Order of the Golden Dawn's *Lesser Banishing Ritual of the Pentagram.*[12]

Originally the name of the "wryneck" bird in Greek literature, which was "bound to a wheel by a sorcerer and spun around as a means of attracting an unfaithful lover," Majercik notes that Iynges are particularly associated with magic.

> In some instances, the wheel itself was called a Iynx. As such, the Iynx functioned as a love charm. Later, under the influence of Plato's spiritualization of Eros, the word Iynx came to mean the "binding" force between man and the gods.[13]

The Iynges are equated with the "thoughts" and thus with the ideas, that is, the Platonic forms of the Paternal Intellect. They are envisaged as "couriers," connected to planetary "Intellectual Supports," operating between the Father and material creation. As such, they are mediating principles that act to bind the intelligible and the sensible.

> The source of the Platonic Forms is the Father, but at his level these Forms remain unified. The Forms become divided at the level of the second Intellect. Once divided into individual Forms, they descend into our world through the World Soul. These Forms, the *Oracle* tells us, are the thoughts of the Father.[14]

"[The] Iynges can be viewed not only as the mediators of messages," Majercik adds in Marshall McLuhan–style,* "but as the message itself."

> For example, as the "thoughts" or Ideas of the Father, the Iynges are actually magical names (*voces mysticae*) sent forth by the Father as "couriers" in order to communicate with the theurgist. At this end, the magic wheel spun by the theurgist attracts these celestial Iynges and enables the theurgist (who alone is privy to the divine language of the gods) to communicate with the Father. But the message communicated by the Iynges is none other than their own magical names which, when uttered, enabled the theurgist to acquire certain divine powers.[15]

One such Iynx-wheel, perhaps the only known in existence, was found at Phaleron and acquired by Boston Museum of Fine Arts in 1928: a four-spoked terracotta wheel surrounded by eleven or twelve long-necked birds in the act of singing, dated to the eighth century BCE,[16] about the time the Homeric epics began being written down.†

While they issue from the Father, the Synocheis, meaning "connectors," differ from the Iynges in that they "harmonize" and "protect" the birdlike messages issuing from the intellect and into the various parts of the created cosmos. Conceivably, they are also possessed of a theurgic function.

> [It] is on the rays of the sun (called "Material Connectors" in fr. 80) that the soul makes its initial ascent. [. . .] This image of the sun with its "connective rays can also serve as a paradigm for the role of the [Synocheis] as a whole: at the theurgic level, the "connective" rays of the sun conduct the soul upward; at the cosmic level, "connective" currents

---

*Marshall McLuhan was a media theorist who coined the phrases *the medium is the message* and *turn on, tune in, drop out*.
†See also the *strophalos* or Hecate's wheel, a circular symbol with a six-pointed star in the center surrounded by a labyrinth.

emanate from the Father, the Primordial Fire, like rays from the sun, disseminating stability and harmony throughout the Universe.[17]

"[This] theurgic dimension," Majercik adds, "is mediated through the Teletarchs."

The lowest in the triad, the Teletarchai, literally meaning "masters of initiation" or "perfection," are concerned with exactly that: perfecting and, through Pistis (Faith), Alêtheia (Truth), and Eros (Love), initiating souls wrapped up in material creation. We have already seen that, for Socrates, Eros is a divine form of madness and, for Diotima, Eros is a great daimon. Alêtheia, on the other hand, is the name of the one, unchanging reality described by the goddess to Parmenides in his underworldly poem. Pistis, finally, who too was personified as a daimona in Greek culture, is envisaged as the very "theurgic power" through which "the theurgist is said to unite with God."

> Indeed, for Proclus, Faith is the supreme virtue, as it is Faith alone, as a "theurgic power" [. . .], which permits union with the One [. . .]. Proclus attributes his understanding of Faith to "the gods" and "the theologians."

Later on, Majercik stresses:

> Proclean Faith [. . .] is a "theurgic power" which unifies the soul and unites it with God. This theurgic dimension, then, clearly links Proclus with the Chaldean tradition, as does his understanding of Faith, Truth, and Love as "purifying" virtues [. . .]
>
> This last emphasis again connects these three virtues with the Teletarchs, as these three rulers are responsible for both purifying the ascending soul of material influences as well as guiding its journey upward.[18]

The Teletarchai are further associated with different regions of the universe. The highest *Teletarch,* Pistis, is associated with the transmundane solar god Aion, located in the empyrean. The ethereal Alêtheia is associated with the mundane solar deity Helios and the planetary realm, while Eros is connected with the moon and sublunary domain. This latter plane is populated with all manner of daimones, ruled over by the lunar Hecate.

Evil daimones are of especial concern in the *Oracles,* which appear in the form of blind hellhounds, "shameless" and "bestial." According to German classicist Helmut Seng, "[the] demons try to disturb the cult of mortals and attempt to deceive them." Fragment 149 says, for example: "When you perceive an earthly demon approaching, offer the *mnizouris* stone while making an invocation."[19] What this "*mnizouris* stone" is we can only guess. But the threat of demonic tampering is clearly a very real concern. Proclus tells us in particular about how "the effluvia of chthonic demons and phantoms become manifest during the holiest of mysteries [. . .], terrifying those who wanted to be initiated, distracting them from the gods' gifts and drawing them toward the material [world]."[20] The word *thuein,* translated as "offer" in fragment 149, means literally "burning for the gods." Stones do not usually incinerate, however.* Tanaseanu-Döbler has the following to say on the matter:

> [T]he idea of [burning] a stone is very rare. [. . .] In order to avoid the strange "sacrifice" of a stone, we might turn to the meaning "fumigation" [which] relies on the very fact that the material in case is burnt releasing vapours and smells. [. . .] One isolated comparandum for this strange sacrifice can be found in the [. . .] Orphic lapidary, the *Lithica,* which was probably composed around the same time as the *Oracles* and recommends the sacrifice of an unidentified stone called [nebritês].[21]

---

*It may be related to *bezoar* stones. The latter are extracted from the bellies of goats that were believed to have eaten serpents. The stone was thought to be the accumulation of the serpents' venom and served as both an antidote for snakebites and as a serpent repellent. The *mnizouris,* similarly, seems to be an apotropaic. Both words appear to be possessed of the same *zour/zoar* root. The word *bezoar* comes from the Persian word *pad-zahr,* which means "antidote," *zahr* meaning "poison." Bezoar stones were largely composed of keratin, which would certainly burn upon incineration. Molten sulphur may also be implied, which Proclus mentions as a means of purification.

The strange *nebritês,* in fact, translated as "jet stone," was directly associated in ancient Greece with epileptic fits.[22] It is notable that, during the Homeric era, epilepsy, which plays an important role in shamanism as well, was believed to be brought on by the gods themselves and was thus called the sacred disease. According to the Christian author Michael Psellos, the sacrifice of the *mnizouris* stone served to summon a daimon that is more powerful than the "demonic dogs."

> This stone has the power to evoke another, greater demon, who will invisibly approach the material demon and proclaim the truth about the questions asked, answering the interrogator. And he utters the evocative name at the same time as the sacrifice of the stone. The Chaldean distinguishes between good and bad demons; but [Christianity] defines that all are evil.[23]

At any rate, warning of these demonic dogs, fragment 135 reads:

> Therefore, even the gods exhort us not to gaze at (these demons) beforehand, until we have been strengthened by the powers from the initiation rites:
> "For you must not gaze at them until you have your body initiated. Being terrestrial, these ill-tempered dogs are shameless."
> And for this reason, the *Oracles* add that
> "they enchant souls, forever turning them away from the rites."[24]

We shall see which "initiation rites" (telestikē) in particular in our examination in chapter 7 of Proclus's Homeric exegesis.

Telestikē can be easily discerned in the *Oracles* where the practice of statue animation is concerned. Still common in the Far East, *prana patishtha,* for instance, is the process by which *prana* or *pneuma* is invoked into a *murti* or cult statue, bringing the same to life. Something of the like may even be found in the *Oracles.* Fragment 224 tells us:

> But execute my statue, purifying it as I shall instruct you. Make a form from wild rue and decorate it with small animals, such as lizards which live about the house. Rub a mixture of myrrh, gum, and frankincense with these animals, and out in the clear air under the waxing moon, complete this (statue) yourself while offering the following prayer.[25]

As indicated above, in addition to statue animation, telestikē may also imply a rite of initiation. In fact, the practices themselves are not too dissimilar. If the process by which a statue is ensouled is applied to a living being, for instance, initiation or perfection is accomplished. If the same is done to an inanimate object, ensoulment appears to be the corresponding result.

That a rite of initiation is implied at some point in the career of the theurgist is clear from fragment 132 of the *Oracles,* which commands "keep silent, initiate."[26] The word *mysta,* translated here as "initiate," is of course borrowed from Eleusis, where it denotes one who has been initiated into the mysteries. And, like in the Eleusinian mysteries, the beginning stages of theurgy involved a katharsis or purification with salt water from the sea. Fragment 133 tells us, for instance:

> Therefore, even the theurgist who conducts this initiation begins with purifications and sprinklings: "Above all, let the priest himself who governs the works of fire, be sprinkled with the icy billow of the deep-roaring sea."[27]

Being an initiatory rite of katharsis, we might name the Greek Orthodox rite of baptism, called *praktikê* by the Christian monk Evagrius of Ponticus (345–399 CE), as a contemporary comparandum. Similar to the Ophian-Christian and *Second Book of Jeu* ascent rituals we will learn about in part two, this particular purgation is followed by an anabasis via the "empyrean channels" of the soul. Fragment 2, one of the most striking in the collection for its unparalleled beauty, reads:

Arrayed from head to toe in a clamorous light, armed in mind and soul with a triple-barbed strength, you must cast into your imagination the entire token of the triad, and not go toward the empyrean channels in a scattered way, but with concentration.[28]

The above excerpt makes reference to something called the "entire token of the triad." We will learn more about tokens or *synthēmata* in chapter 8.

Taken alone, the *Oracles'* injunction to "not go toward the empyrean channels in a scattered way" but to do so with "concentration" doesn't mean much. But this injunction combined with a potential allusion to ritualized breathing in fragment 124 ("Those who, by inhaling, drive out the soul, are free"[29]) has perhaps inevitably suggested to some scholars a connection to the yogic practices of dharana (concentration) and pranayama (controlled breathing)—as unconventional as this juxtapositioning might be. Running parallel to this reading is the view of John M. Dillon that theurgy may in fact be a distant relative of Transcendental Meditation techniques known from Eastern religions. "[A] crucial part seems to have been played by light," Dillon believes, "which was visualized as illuminating the soul from all about, filling it with fire and uniting it to the gods."

Radek Chlup, a lecturer at Charles University, Prague, observed that "we may thus expect the basic procedure to revolve around 'a series of spiritual exercises based on the contemplation of images of light' [. . .], possibly accompanied by appropriate bodily techniques, such as a special style of breathing."[30] In Chlup's view,

the light that was the object of the theurgist's contemplation would probably assume a more specific form than it did in the meditations of Plotinus, conforming to some standard symbolic patterns. [In] view of Proclus' henadology we may presume that the unique individuality of each of the gods would also have played its part, each vision being colored according to the attributes of the particular divinity worshipped. [. . .] Indeed, since the inborn *synthēma* that each soul is supposed to be present to the Father is unique for each individual, depending on the divine chain to which he or she belongs [. . .] it is probable that the exact visions used would differ from person to person.[31]

On the subject of soul ascent, fragments 110 and 115 continue:

Seek out the channel of the soul, from where it [descended] in a certain order to serve the body; [and] seek [how] you will raise it up again to its order by combining (ritual) action with a sacred word.[32]

You must hasten toward the light and toward the rays of the Father, from where the soul, clothed in mighty intellect, has been sent to you.[33]

The comparisons with the Mithras Liturgy are numerous and instructive. *PGM* IV.538 begins, for example, with the following instructions:

Draw in [pneuma] from the rays, drawing up 3 times as much as you can, and you will see yourself being lifted up and / ascending to the height, so that you seem to be in midair.[34]

Emperor Julian (331–363 CE), the so-called apostate, writes of these same elevating "rays" in his *Hymn to King Helios* when he says:

For from him [i.e., Helios] we are born, and by him we are nourished. But his more divine gifts, and all that he bestows on our souls when he frees them from the body and then lifts them on high to the region of those substances that are akin to the god; and the fineness and vigor of his divine rays, which are assigned as a sort of vehicle for the safe descent of our souls into this world of generation.[35]

These "divine rays," which, Julian says, "are assigned as a sort of vehicle for the safe descent of our souls into this world of generation," clearly allude to the pneumatic ochēma, referenced above.

As Johnston observes, the use of the words *hiereus,* translated in the above fragment (fragment 133) as "priest," and *mystês,* translated as "initiate" in the fragment quoted immediately before (fragment 135), would seem to imply a group of working theurgists, as opposed to simply solo practitioners—even if the majority of the work may have been done one on one. The first example of this type of dynamic relationship would be the Juliani themselves, the theurgist son having likely learned these rites from his father, the Chaldæan. Similarly, the emperor Julian, the so-called apostate—not to be confused with the aforementioned Juliani—was privately instructed in theurgy by Maximus of Ephesus, a student of Aedesius, who himself was pupil to none other than Iamblichus.* According to Johnston, Aedesius was a close friend of the mysterious figure of Sosipatra of Pergamum. Along with her son, the philosopher Antoninus, Sosipatra was not only a practicing theurgist and philosopher but was also a powerful oracle. We might also mention in this regard Proclus, who was initiated into theurgy by Asclepigeneia, the daughter of the theurgist Plutarch, who in turn learned from his father, the theurgist Nestorius. The criteria of "esoteric transmission"[36] of the late Antoine Faivre, a French scholar of Western esotericism, immediately comes to mind and would very much apply to the lineal descents of our theurgic practitioners. The ritual recorded in the Mithras Liturgy, not unlike Plutarch to Asclepigeneia, is passed on from a father to his daughter as well.

Sosipatra's story is interesting enough to warrant a small aside at the close of this chapter. At the age of five, two men, suggested by

---

*Iamblichus was said to have been able to levitate more than fifteen feet off the ground. During this impossible feat, his body and garments would "change to a beautiful golden hue." According to Eunapius, while bathing at a natural spring with his disciples, Iamblichus was asked to make a demonstration of his powers. He proceeded to ascertain from the locals of the area the original names by which two small hot springs located within the vicinity were known by the natives in olden times. Touching the waters, whispering an unknown invocation, Iamblichus summoned two beautiful boys, Eros and Arteros, from their respective springs. Eros "was white-skinned and of medium height, his locks were golden and his back and breast shone." Anteros resembled Eros "in all respects, except that his hair was darker and fell loose in the sun." Both boys embraced Iamblichus as though he were their father.

Eunapius (347–ca. 414 CE), a Greek sophist and historian, to be daimones or perhaps even the reincarnated Juliani themselves, who said that
they were not "uninitiated in the wisdom called Chaldean," showed
up unannounced and asked Sosipatra's father if they could tend to his
young daughter and, over the course of the next five years, educate and
initiate her into the Chaldæan mysteries while he was away. Upon her
father's return, Eunapius says, she was unrecognizable to him. The two
strangers invited the dumbfounded man to ask her anything he wished
as a proof of Sosipatra's thorough learning and comprehension of "the
books of the poets, philosophers, and orators," which, we are told, were
constantly "on her lips." But, to the contrary, the girl interjected saying,
"Rather ask instead, father, what happened to you on the road."

> She described his journey to him in accurate detail "as if she had
> been holding the reins," for he traveled in a four-wheeled car-
> riage, a luxury conveyance that was prone to many calamities. [. . .]
> Sosipatra's father was amazed by her report and concluded that she
> must be a goddess.[37]

When the men departed, they left Sosipatra with her initiatory robes,
various instruments (including perhaps an Iynx-wheel), and a collection
of small books—all of which could fit inside a tiny chest.

As Dillon has shown, based on the appearance of certain "striking
turns of phrase,"[38] there is evidence that Plotinus was very likely familiar
with the *Chaldæan Oracles* and had at least perused them. In any case,
his writings in the *Enneads* on mystical union with the One provide us
with valuable insight into the internal components of theurgic ritual. It
is therefore to the author of the *Enneads,* the first Neoplatonist proper,
that we now turn in search of motifs that would go on to be influential
among theurgists. Like the Hermetica discussed in chapter 5, Plotinus
doesn't figure too largely into our study, but for the sake of being thematically comprehensive, he does at least deserve some mention as a
para-Homeric source for Porphyry and Proclus, for Plotinus's influence
on later Neoplatonism and theurgy is both formidable and undeniable.

4

PLOTINUS AND THE PLATONIZING SETHIAN GNOSTICS

A Look at the Father of Neoplatonism and His Precarious Relationship with the Sethian School of Gnosticism

A Roman Egyptian by birth, Plotinus studied under the philosophical autodidact Ammonius Saccas and became the father of Neoplatonism when he authored a series of nine tractates titled the *Enneads,* which laid the foundations for later Platonism(s). Central to Plotinus's philosophy is an idea that we have encountered repeatedly in our study, what the late Alexander J. Mazur, an American scholar who specialized in Neoplatonism, Gnosticism, and mysticism, refers to as MUO or "mystical union with the One." However, Mazur indicated that one cannot discuss Plotinus's mysticism without also writing about a late antique fringe demographic that has come to be known as the Platonizing Sethian Gnostics,[1] whose texts betray more than a passing familiarity—nay, a veritable appropriation—on the part of Plotinus. This is not without a hint of irony as Plotinus outright rejected the Gnostics in chapter 9 of *Ennead* II, frankly titled "Against the Gnostics."[2] Porphyry provides us with some background in *On the Life of Plotinus,* his biography of his master:

> During [Plotinus's] lifetime, Christianity attracted a diverse popular following, as did movements which drew on ancient philosophy. Followers of Adelphius and Aquilinus got hold of most of the writings of Alexander of Lybia, Philocomus, Demostratus, and Lydus, and published the revelations of Zoroaster, Zostrianos, Nicotheus, Allogenes, and Messus. There were others of the sort. They deceived many people—indeed, they were themselves deluded. As if Plato had not come to grips with the profundity of intelligible substance! Plotinus himself refuted them on many points in the course of our seminars, and he wrote a book which we called *Against the Gnostics* [II.9]; but he left it to us to judge the rest. Amelius managed to write 40 books against the *Book of Zostrianos.* I, Porphyry, composed a continuous series of arguments against the *Book of Zoroaster,* proving beyond doubt that it is a recent forgery, fabricated by the sect's adherents to give the impression that the doctrines they themselves approve are those of the ancient Zoroaster.[3]

Two of the documents mentioned by Porphyry, *Zostrianos* and *Allogenes,* were discovered among the Gnostic texts found in Nag Hammadi in 1945, known as the Nag Hammadi Library. Similar to the Jewish Hekhalot and apocalyptic literature, *Zostrianos* and *Allogenes* each describe the ascents of eponymous visionaries toward the "utterly ineffable, unknowable deity,"[4] that is, the One, descriptions that very much resemble the mystical reversion outlined by Plotinus. Moreover, the theological structure in *Zostrianos* makes use of the same being-life-mind triad first intimated by Plotinus and familiar to later Neoplatonists. Furthermore, Zostrianos, it is notable, was the parent of Armenios, said by Plato in the *Republic* to be the father of the hero in the "Myth of Er."[5]

Other Platonizing texts in circulation among the Sethian Gnostics that were found in the Nag Hammadi cache include the *Three Steles* *of Seth,* which Mazur holds also had an effect on the development of Plotinus's mysticism, and *Marsanes.* Notably, in these two and in the *Gospel of the Egyptians*—known also as the *Holy Book of the Great Invisible Spirit,* another Platonizing Sethian Nag Hammadi text that is not to be confused with the similarly titled *Greek Gospel of the Egyptians*—Birger A. Pearson, an American scholar studying early Christianity and Gnosticism,* had already identified "theurgic tendencies"[6] per the definitions contained in Iamblichus's *De mysteriis.* Gregory Shaw informs us that "since the Gnostics did not provide a theoretical framework to explain their rites and Iamblichus did not provide concrete ritual data, Pearson's study is useful for both scholars of Gnosticism and later Neoplatonism."[7]

The general consensus regarding Plotinus has been that he was less concerned with ritual than with purely contemplative, philosophical ascent. But, "it is possible to develop a theory of theurgy from one side of the thought of Plotinus," A. H. Armstrong assures us (A. H. Armstrong, "Tradition, Reason, and Experience in the Thought of Plotinus," Plotinian and Christian Studies 17 (London: Variorum reprints, 1979), 187). As historian Crystal Addey has argued,[8] just because Plotinus's *epistrophe* is structured as an internal process and involves no known physical movements, paraphernalia, or invocations doesn't make it any less ritualized. To quote Radek Chlup:

> [There] is no reason to see [Plotinus's contemplative techniques] as sharply distinguished from external ritual operations.[9] [. . .]
>
> [The] spiritual exercises of Plotinus were ritualized in one regard, namely that they had a strong performative dimension. [. . .] In this respect, Plotinus' techniques of ascent were probably related to the highest types of theurgy.[10]

The meditative rituals of Vajrayana Buddhism are a fitting comparandum. Moreover, the picture of Plotinus as dismissive of ritual in general is inconsistent with the account of his pupil, Porphyry, in the latter's work *On the Life of Plotinus.*

---

*We will return to the Gnostics in chapter 6.

An Egyptian priest once came to Rome and met [Plotinus] through a mutual friend. Wanting to give a demonstration of his wisdom, he invited Plotinus to come and see him summon his guardian daemon. Plotinus readily agreed, and the invocation took place in the temple of Isis, since the Egyptian said that this was the only pure place he could find in Rome. When he called upon Plotinus' daemon to appear, it was a god that came, rather than a member of the genus of daemons. As the Egyptian said: "You are blessed, since you have a god as your daemon, and are not accompanied by a member of the lower genus." They were not able to ask or learn more while it was there, since one of their friends, who was watching with them, strangled the birds he was holding as protection—whether deliberately, through envy, or in a moment of panic. In any case, the fact that Plotinus was accompanied by a daemon of superior divinity led him to raise his god-like vision towards it. This is why he wrote the book *On Our Allotted Daemon* [3.4], in which he tries to explain why different people have different guardians.[11]

Far from a rejection, here we have a chapter from Plotinus's own *Enneads* allegedly being inspired by nothing short of a ritual performance. This should call into question the image of Plotinus as being opposed to ritual as a whole, for it is within the context of an internalized ritual that we believe Plotinus's systematic process of mystical union with the One should be viewed. According to Porphyry, his master attained said union, while in his presence, on at least four separate occasions.[12]

Plotinus made distinctions among three different classes of souls. There exist those who make no effort to rise above the material plane, those who try to ascend and fail, and then there are those stubborn souls who, like the theurgists, succeed and arrive at the intelligible realm "as if after much wandering a human being arrived in his well-governed fatherland."[13] Here, as Algis Uždavinys observes, Plotinus quietly makes Odysseus "a symbol of the highest class of humanity—those philosophers and mystics who have reached their spiritual Home."[14] Quoting *Iliad* II.140, Plotinus writes in an earlier *Ennead:*

"[Let] us flee to our beloved fatherland." But what is this flight, how is it accomplished? Let us set sail in the way Homer, in an allegorical way, I think, tells us that Odysseus fled from the sorceress Circe or from Calypso. Odysseus was not satisfied to remain there, even though he had visual pleasures and passed his time with sensual beauty. Our fatherland, from where we have actually come, and our father are both in the intelligible world.[15]

In theory, Plotinus's process of mystical union with the One should be a veritable reversal of his ontology, that is, collapsing the soul's own ontological emanation back into her *pēgē* source. However, in his research, Mazur identified a discrepancy in the practice of Plotinus's process of mystical reversion that can only be explained by referring to the writings of the Sethian Gnostics, which were making their rounds in Plotinus's circle.

A very simplified account of Plotinus's philosophy at the level of the three hypostases is as follows. The Monad, which is beyond both being and mind, is possessed of a certain fullness—an *energeia*—that, while transcending space and time, nonetheless somehow overflows in a divine efflux. When this overflow reverts, it contemplates itself and nous or mind then comes into being. When the overflow of nous in turn contemplates itself, psyche or soul emerges. Thus are generated the three hypostases: Monad, nous (mind), and psyche (soul). As a rule, although atemporal, nous must come "after" the Monad in the order of hypostatic emergence, allowing for no intermediaries. The same is true of psyche in regard to nous; although as we're about to find out, in his process of mystical union with the One, Plotinus necessarily breaks this rule and posits an intermediary placeholder between nous and the Monad. Mazur calls this intermediary, "prenoetic efflux"[16] and relates it to the second and third stages in Plotinus's process of mystical union with the One, labeled *Mystical Self-Reversion* and *Autophony*—stages that appear in both *Zostrianos* and *Allogenes* and quoted by Porphyry. They also appear in the *Three Steles of Seth*.

According to Mazur, the phases of Plotinus's process of mystical union with the One are five in number, with a sixth subphase following the third. Mazur terms Phase A *catharsis* and notes that "Plotinus frames the entire ascent as a cathartic process in which the soul sloughs off its extraneous accretions so as to reveal an essentially divine core."

> This appears to involve both a cognitive aspect—the purification of one's conception of the One from any contamination with multiplicity, including one's awareness of the formal delimitations of Intellect or lesser ontological strata—and a corresponding ontological aspect—the dismissal from one's own self (the locus of mystical subjectivity) of any thought, any knowledge, and indeed, any mental activity whatsoever.[17]

Phase B, called *mystical self-reversion,* is described by Mazur as "an acute, reflexive re-focusing or concentration of awareness upon itself or, more metaphorically, an 'inward' reversion towards the essential core of the self." In this phase, the mystical aspirant "seems to be a labile faculty of the individual that is described either as the soul having assimilated itself to the hypostatic Intellect, or instead, as a special modality of the Intellect itself."[18] This is precisely where things get complicated. In Phase C, mystical self-reversion culminates in a "sudden [. . .] experience of [. . .] a luminous vision, a vision whose object most often is not the goal (that is, the One itself) but rather, one's own self." Mazur calls this self-manifestation the *autophany.*[19] It is this phase that corresponds most closely with Plotinus's anomalous "prenoetic efflux." In Phase C, *self-unification,* Plotinus "exhorts one to coalesce with the beautiful image of oneself and thus attain the superior unity of complete self-identity, in a preliminary unification that almost always precedes [. . .] the ultimate union with the One."[20] In Phase D, however, Plotinus insists that "even this self, too, must be rejected in a terminal moment of utter self-negation, dissolution, surrender, or displacement." Mazur calls this penultimate phase *annihilation.*[21] The final phase, *union with the One,* then constitutes "an absolute unification, coalescence, or even identity of the mystical aspirant and the One."[22] While the process involves no physical gestures, invocations, or ritual paraphernalia, it is clear that Plotinus's protocols for mystical union with the One are no less of a ritual.

Furthermore, as Addey has observed, Plotinus exhibits a generally positive attitude toward ritual practices, especially in regard to his discussion of telestikē in terms of statue animation. Plotinus writes in *Ennead* IV.3.11.1–7:

> It seems to me that the sages of old who wanted to attract to themselves the presence of the gods, and built [. . .] statues to that end, looking to the nature of the universe, had in mind that the nature of the soul is a thing that is in general easy to attract, but the easiest way of all to receive it would be if one were to craft something sympathetic which was able to receive some share of it. And that is sympathetic which is in any way imitative of it, like a mirror able to catch some image of it.[23]

We return to the topic of statue animation in chapter 8.

Toward the end of his Plotinian biography, Porphyry tells his reader of what became of the postmortem soul of his beloved master, which Amelius learned from an oracle of Apollo. The fate of Plotinus's soul in this account is reminiscent of the charioteer in Plato's *Phaedrus,* wrestling with two winged horses, one mortal and one immortal. It is notable that one line in particular was directly inspired by Homer's *Odyssey* V.388–450: "from the tempestuous waves of embodiment you [i.e., Plotinus] had strength to swim, to reach the headland's shores." We shall see in chapter 6 that the Neoplatonists regarded Homer's "wine-dark sea" as an apt symbol for *genesis* and the realm of the cosmos—from which Odysseus (and Plotinus) is to be ultimately liberated.

> Amelius asked Apollo where the soul of Plotinus had gone—Apollo who simply said of Socrates: "Socrates is the wisest of all men."
> Listen to what he said, and at what great length, about Plotinus:

[. . .] Daemon, that were a man before, entering now a diviner rank: you became a daemon, when you loosed the chain of necessity that is the human being's lot; and from the tempestuous waves of embodiment had strength to swim, to reach the headland's shores, far from the shoals of the sinful. You set your foot on the sinuous path laid out for the pure in soul, where the light of the gods and their laws show the way, innocent of, rising above, the lawlessness of the sinful.

While twisting to flee the bitter waves, where blood sustains and whirlpools menace, mid-torrent, amid deafening confusion, the god-sent goal would often be made to seem near. Often the darts which your intellect fired were borne by their very strength along deviant paths: the gods then, shone focused rays of light which helped you to see from the gloomy shade, and raised you straight to the circling, deathless path. The pleasure of sleep never wholly took hold of your eyes, the heavy bolt of its mist not allowed to seal your lids, so that, borne through the whirlpools, your eyes remained opened to many and joyful things, things sought with difficulty by men who go after wisdom.

But now that you have struck your tent, and left the grave of a daemon-soul, you come along the assembly of daemons refreshed by the lovely breezes: where love is, where beautiful yearning is, full of pure joy, always replenished by deathless streams from god. From here come the reins of loves; from here the sweet breeze and calmness of aether. Here live the brothers of the golden generation of great Zeus: Minos and Rhadamanthus. Here lives the just Aeacus; here are Plato's holy strength, and the beautiful Pythagoras, and those who started the dance of immortal love and won for themselves a common lineage with the most blessed daemons. Here the heart in good cheer is always warned and cheerful. Oh blessed one, how many contests you have endured! Go now among holy daemons, your turbid lives the crest on your helmet.[24]

5

HERMETICA AND THEURGY

*A Discussion on the Emergence of Hermetism
with Reference to Its Close Parallels with the
Art of Theurgy*

Hermetism, a syncretic religion born from the meeting of Egypt and Greece in the forms of the gods, Thoth or Tehuti and Hermes Trismegistus, is conveniently divided into two camps: *Hermetism* proper and *Hermeticism*. Hermetism refers to the Hermetic tradition at the time that it flourished—before the fall of the Byzantine Empire. Hermeticism, then, alludes to the resurrection of the Hermetic tradition after its rediscovery by the likes of Marcilio Ficino and Ludovico Lazzarelli in the Florentine Academy in the fifteenth century.

The original Hermetism may be further divided into two subgenres: *philosophical* and *technical*. The former concerns theoretical documents like the *Corpus Hermeticum, Asclepius,* and the writings of Stobaeus, while the latter includes practical texts such as the famous *Tabula Smaragdina* or *Emerald Tablet*, the *Discourse on the Eighth and Ninth,* and the *Prayer of Thanksgiving* (the latter an epilogue to the *Discourse on the Eighth and Ninth*) from the Nag Hammadi Library; the second-century alchemical manuscript *Isis the Prophetess to Her Son Horus;* the astrological *Liber Hermetis,* which contains elements that are datable to the second century BCE; and certain texts from the *Papyri Graecae Magicae* that cite Hermes as a source. Some good examples of the latter are *PGM* IV.2737–440, a rite of statue animation labeled "Charm for acquiring business and for calling in customers,"[1] and *PGM* V.213–303, called "Hermes' ring."[2]

Hermeticism, on the other hand, reached its fullest fruition in the infamous magical orders of the nineteenth-century occult revival, the Hermetic Brotherhood of Luxor and the Hermetic Order of the Golden Dawn. The former was based largely on the tantra-like teachings of Paschal Beverly Randolph, who edited an edition of *Hermes Mercurius Trismegistus: His Divine Pymander* in 1871. The latter was founded by three magi from the Masonic Rosicrucian Society, *Societas Rosicruciana in Anglia,* one of whom, William Wynn Westcott, published, in 1894, *The Chaldæan Oracles of Zoroaster,* translated by Thomas Taylor, volume 6 of his *Collectanea Hermetica* series. It is Hermetism proper that will concern us here.

As Gregory Shaw has pointed out, while the Hermetica is a class of literature distinct from that of the theurgists, the two traditions are nonetheless linked as examples of practices aimed at planetary ascent and the immortalization of the soul. "The writings of theurgic Platonists and Hermetists share a common purpose," notes Shaw, "to make the soul immortal and divine."[3] "Sharply dividing the theurgists from the Hermeticists falsely represents ancient reality," says Sarah Iles Johnston, for "'theurgy' and 'Hermeticism' were two names for essentially the same constellation of beliefs and practices."

Ancient authors sometimes traced what they called Hermetic beliefs to Egypt, and traced beliefs expressed in the *Chaldean Oracles,* of course, to Chaldea, but even these geographic labels were applied fluidly, and we would be wrong to impose strict divisions between one and the other.[4]

Moreover, in his challenging defense of theurgy, *De mysteriis,* Iamblichus begins Book I of his dissertation with a reference to none other than Hermes, "patron of all priests."

> Hermes, the god who presides over rational discourse, has long been considered, quite rightly, to be the common patron of all priests; he who presides over true knowledge about the gods is one and the same always and everywhere. It is to him that our ancestors in particular dedicated the fruits of their wisdom, attributing all their own writings to Hermes.[5]

For Iamblichus, regardless of the particular religion, the theurgist is a type of universal priest, and Hermes Trismegistus, his deific *arche* or primal source of action.

In addition to their arrangement after the form of a traditional Platonic dialogue, with Hermes Trismegistus playing the role of Socrates instructing his son or pupil Tat (Thoth?) in the ways of Hermetic philosophy, there are a number of other motifs in the *Corpus Hermeticum* with which the Platonist will no doubt be familiar. Chapter 1, for example, titled, "Poimandres," outlines the method of ascent back into the Ogdoad, beyond the fatal causality of the seven planets.

> First, in releasing the material body you give the body itself over to alteration, and the form that you used to have vanishes. To the demon you give over your temperament, now inactive. The body's senses rise up and flow back to their particular sources, becoming separate parts and mingling again with the energies. And feeling and longing go on toward irrational nature. Thence the human being rushes up through the cosmic framework, at the first zone surrendering the energy of increase and decrease; at the second evil machination, a device now inactive; at the third the illusion of longing, now inactive; at the fourth the ruler's arrogance, now freed of excess; at the fifth unholy presumption and daring recklessness; at

the sixth the evil impulses that come from wealth, now inactive; and at the seventh zone the deceit that lies in ambush. And then, stripped of the effects of the cosmic framework, the human enters the region of the ogdoad; he has his own proper power, and along with the blessed he hymns the father. Those present there rejoice in his presence, and, having become like his companions, he also hears certain powers that exist beyond the ogdoadic region [i.e., in the *Ennead*] and hymn god with sweet voice. They rise up to the father in order and surrender themselves to the powers, and, having become powers, they enter into god. This is the final good for those who have received knowledge: to be made god.[6]

From their characteristics, we can ascertain that the order of the planets here is that of the Ptolemaic model. "[Energy] of increase and decrease" refers to the traditional traits of the moon, which controls the ebb and flow of sublunary existence, while "evil machination" alludes to the scheming plots of Mercury, the god of thieves. The "illusion of longing" is a clear indication of the characteristics of Venus, as is the "ruler's arrogance" of prideful Sol. "[Unholy] presumption and daring recklessness" suggests the arrogant temerity of the planet Mars, in the same way that "evil impulses that come from wealth" is suggestive of the excesses of planet Jupiter. Finally, the "deceit that lies in ambush" must be an allusion to the planet Saturn.

In his remarkable new book, *Hermetic Spirituality and the Historic Imagination: Altered States of Knowledge in Late Antiquity*, Wouter Hanegraaff, a Dutch professor of history of Hermetic philosophy, found it helpful to pair each above-mentioned vice with its corresponding virtue.

As the soul transcends the domain of the lunar sphere, it is no longer afflicted by restless change but moves into a state of peaceful stability. As it transcends the dominion of Mercury, the "machinery of corruption" [. . .] loses its power so that goodness can take its place. As the soul ceases to be influenced by Venus, it can no longer be led astray by sexual desires. Leaving the sphere of the Sun behind, its addiction to power vanishes too. The reckless brutality of violence that comes from Mars gives way to the energy of peace. Leaving Jupiter's dominion, the soul is no longer addicted to material possessions either. And as it finally leaves Saturn behind too, it turns its back on deceit and embraces truth. [. . .] This enables it to enter the Ogdoad, where it is joyfully welcomed by the other ascended souls.[7]

At each of the seven planetary heavens, not unlike Plotinus's process of mystical union with the One, Hermes frames the entire ascent as a cathartic process wherein the soul "sloughs off its extraneous accretions so as to reveal an essentially divine core."[8] It is remarkable that, for the ancient Egyptians, the Ogdoad and Ennead were primordial classes of deities intimately associated with the god Thoth for a number of centuries. This has led to Thoth being called "the lord of the city of the Eight"—that is, Hermopolis-Ashmouneïn (from the Coptic *šmoun,* meaning "eight")—or the "lord of the Ennead."[9] By the time we encounter the theurgists, however, these classes will have been translated into purely planetary and stellar terms.

Chapter 8 of the *Corpus Hermeticum,* on the other hand, titled "That none of the things that are is destroyed, and they are mistaken who say that changes are deaths and destructions," paints a picture for the reader that very much resembles that of the Demiurge in Plato's *Timaeus.* "God is in reality the first of all entities, eternal, unbegotten, Craftsman [Demiurge] of the whole of existence," verse two starts, followed by a clear allusion to Plato's "Allegory of the Cave":

And the father [took the matter that he desired] to set aside and made it all into a spherical form with body and bulk. The matter that he invested with this spherical quality is immortal, and its materiality is eternal. Further, the father implanted in the sphere the qualities of forms, shutting them up as in a cave.[10]

And, we have already seen in our introduction that the Demiurge's krater is recast in chapter 4 of the *Corpus* as a "mixing bowl [of] mind" or nous, titled "The Mixing Bowl or the Monad."

> He filled a great mixing bowl with [mind] and sent it below, appointing a herald whom he commanded to make the following proclamation to human hearts: "Immerse yourself in the mixing bowl if your heart has the strength, if it believes you will rise up again to the one who sent the mixing bowl below, it recognizes the purpose of your coming to be."[11]

Again, this Hermetic, baptismal imagery recurs in the Hellenistic alchemical tract the *Visions of Zosimos*.

Where the *Corpus Hermeticum* is more on the philosophical side, the *Discourse on the Eighth and Ninth* from the Nag Hammadi discovery is instead a technical instruction on the ritualized ascent of the soul into the Ogdoad and beyond. The rite begins with "Prayer for the Ascent to the Eighth and Ninth." One would be forgiven for mistaking the divine recipient of the following prayer for Plato's Demiurge, for his "will produces life for the forms everywhere," and his "nature gives form to substance;" from him, "the universe received soul."

> *I call upon you,*
> *who rules over the kingdom of power,*
> *whose word is an offspring of light,*
> *whose words are immortal,*
> *eternal, immutable,*
> *whose will produces life for the forms everywhere,*
> *whose nature gives form to substance,*
> *by whom souls, [powers], and angels are moved,*
> *[whose] word [reaches all] who exist,*
> *whose forethought reaches everyone [in] that [place],*
> *[who] produces everyone,*
> *who has [divided] the eternal realm among spirits,*

who has created everything,
who, being self within self, supports everything,
being perfect,
the invisible God to whom one speaks in silence,
whose image is moved when it is managed,
and it is so managed,
mighty one in power,
who is exalted above majesty,
who is superior to those honored,

[ΖѠƷΛΘΛΖѠ

Λ

ѠѠ ЄЄ

ѠѠѠ ΗΗΗ

ѠѠѠ Ѡ ΗΗ

ѠѠѠѠѠѠ ΟΟΟΟΟ

ѠѠѠѠѠѠ ΥΥΥΥΥΥ

ѠѠѠѠѠѠѠѠѠѠѠ ѠѠѠ

ΖѠΖΛΖѠΘ]*

Lord, grant us wisdom from your power that
    reaches us,
that we may relate to ourselves the vision of the eighth
    and ninth.
Already we have advanced to the seventh,
since we are faithful
and abide in your law.
Your will we fulfill always.
We have walked in [your way]
[and have] renounced [evil],
so the vision may come.
Lord, grant us truth in the image.
Grant that through spirit we may see
the form of the image that lacks nothing,

---

*Vowels corrected by Brian P. Alt.

and accept the reflection of the [Plêrôma]*
from us through our praise.
Recognize the spirit within us.
From you the universe received soul.
From you, one unbegotten,
the begotten one came to be.
The birth of the self-begotten is through you,
the birth of all begotten things that exist.
Accept these spiritual offerings from us,
which we direct to you
with all our heart, soul, and strength.
Save what is within us,
and grant us immortal wisdom.[12]

The apparently nonsensical string of untranslated vowels framed by the two *nomina barbara* (literally *barbarous names,* meaning "incomprehensible words") in the middle of the prayer are known as *vōcēs magicae* (magical words) and allude to the process of planetary ascent into the Ogdoad and Ennead used by the Hermetists. According to the Pythagorean teachings of Nicomachus of Gerasa, the vowels are unspeakable and relate to the consonants as does the soul to the body. Moreover, the seven vowels correspond to the seven planets known to the ancients, from Luna to Saturn. Thus, as Christian Hervik Bull, a Norwegian researcher of late antiquity and professor of religion, discovered, the two *etas* in the string should in fact be four *iotas*. The final *omega,* then, has a double correlation of both Saturn and Oceanus—the latter of which is connected to the realm of the fixed stars as "that which encircles and surrounds the cosmos."

The Ocean encircled the entire world in Greek mythology, with all constellations and stars diving into it, and it is therefore a suitable

---

*[Here,] the term *plêrôma* refers to the fullness of the cosmos, not the immaterial supracosmic realm" (Bull, "Monkey Business," 75–94).

symbol of the outer limit of the Ptolemaic spherical cosmos, girding the fixed stars.[13]

In regard to the double function of the omega, the two levels of interpretation are actually attested by Zosimus of Panopolis. "First, as the seventh vowel the omega denotes the seventh planetary cycle of Saturn," Bull reiterates, and second, "it denotes Ocean [. . .] as the first letter in that name, and as such is the birth and seed of all gods." This, Bull concludes significantly, is "likely a Homeric echo." The remaining thirty-six omegas that are dispersed throughout the planetary vowels, on the other hand, refer to the thirty-six decans of the Egyptian astrological system. And the twenty-eight planetary vowels (one vowel is added at each successive line, i.e., *A / EE / HHH / IIII*, etc.) taken together suggest the twenty-eight days of the lunar month.

We do not know exactly how these names were spoken or intoned, but the effect must certainly have been impressive, resulting in a solemn ceremonial atmosphere pregnant with expectation. [. . .] An important point that has not received enough attention is that next to being linked to the planetary spheres, the seven vowels could also be mapped on one of the musical scales or "modes." According to Neopythagorean theory as explained notably in Nicomachus of Gerasa's influential books on harmonics (later first/early second cent. CE), each planet rotating through the ether was continually producing a specific tonal pitch. As a logical inference, the seven planetary vowels could be linked to the seven tones of the existing musical scales as well. [. . .] Since we do not know which one(s) would have been used by Hermetic practitioners, all we can say with confidence is that the scale would run from omega (Saturn) as the lowest tone to alpha (moon) as the highest.[14]

Finally, the nomina barbara *ZOXATHAZO ZOZAZOTH* may refer to a scene in the *Leiden Kosmopoïia,* where the creator god is said to have laughed seven times, each laugh producing a new divine hypostasis. "The fourth hypostasis is Creative Force which governs Procreation, *Genna* and *Spora* in Greek, which we recognize as the epithets of Ocean in the Homeric passage quoted by Zosimus," Bull explains. "These hypostases are also given the *nomina barbara* [*BADETOPHOTH ZOTHAXATHOZ*], the latter of which is a close approximation of the *nomina* of *Disc. 8–9*, [*ZOXATHAZO*] and [*ZOZAZOTH*]."[15] Hanegraaff offers another possibility.

> The first and final word, *zōxathazō* and *zōzazōth,* have no literal parallels elsewhere in Greek or Coptic literature but are reminiscent of well-known palindromes that occur in the Greek "magical" papyri and contemporary "magical" amulets, notably *zōthaxathōz* and *thōzaxazōth.* That the version in [the *Discourse on the Eighth and Ninth*] are not palindromes is unlikely to be the result of transcription errors—most probably we are dealing with a deliberate attempt to make the formula ineffective for non-initiate readers. After all, the authors were extremely serious in their belief that these sounds would unleash real and supremely sacred energetic power.[16]

Remarkably, the group of Hermetists responsible for the *Discourse on the Eighth and Ninth* actually go so far as to indicate in the text the precise astrological election for their rite of initiation into the highest spheres: "when Mercury was in the house of Virgo and the sun was in the first half of the day and fifteen degrees had passed by Mercury"[17]—that is, as close as the planet can get to the sun without going "combust."

We saw in the introduction in regard to the technical (as opposed to philosophical) Hermetica that Hermetism does not concern itself solely with the anagogic variety of theurgy, but even makes recourse to telestikē in the form of statue animation. Chapters 23 to 24 of the Latin *Asclepius,* for example, read as follows:

> [T]he figures of gods that humans form have been formed of both natures—from the divine [. . .] and the material of which they are built. [. . .] Always mindful of its nature and origin, humanity

persists in imitating divinity. [. . .] I mean statues ensouled and conscious, filled with spirit and doing great deeds; statues that foreknow the future and predict it by lots, by prophecy, by dreams and by many other means; statues that make people ill and cure them, bringing them pain and pleasure as each deserves.[18]

Chapters 37 and 38 continue this discussion:

[It] exceeds the wonderment of all wonders that humans have been able to discover the divine nature and how to make it. Our ancestors [. . .] discovered the art of making gods. To their discovery they added a conformable power arising from the nature of matter. Because they could not make souls, they mixed this power in and called up the souls of demons or angels and implanted them in likenesses through holy and divine mysteries, whence the idols could have the power to do good and evil. [. . .] It comes from a mixture of plants, stones and spices [. . .] that have in them a natural power of divinity. And this is why those gods are entertained with constant sacrifices, with hymns, praises and sweet sounds in tune with heaven's harmony: so that the heavenly ingredient enticed into the idol by constant communication with heaven may gladly endure its long stay among mankind. Thus does man fashion his gods.[19]

As noted earlier, we will get much deeper into the subject of telestikē and statue animation in chapter 8.

In terms of Porphyry's and Proclus's para-Homeric sources, we have seen that the shamans, *iatromanteia,* and Presocratics basically set the stage for later theurgic developments. By the time we get to Plato, the orientation of soul flight has shifted from katabasis to anabasis, and we're reintroduced to the imagery of the Parmenidean soul chariot in Plato's *Phaedrus* that will figure later in the philosophy of the Neoplatonists. In the *Chaldæan Oracles,* we saw the development of Platonic philosophy into a veritable theology based on theurgy proper, and with Plotinus and the Platonizing Sethian Gnostics, we were initiated into the anomalous process of mystical union with the One. Finally, we found that the Hermetica, while distinct from theurgy, is nonetheless analogous to it as a Hellenistic tradition of soul immortalization aimed at union with the deity. We will now turn to part two of our study in search of theoretical, theurgic elements, which Porphyry identified within Homer's epic poem the *Odyssey*.

*At the head of the harbor, there is an olive tree with spreading
leaves, and nearby is a cave that is shaded, and pleasant,
and sacred to the nymphs who are called the Nymphs of the
    Wellsprings,
Naiads. There are mixing bowls and handled jars inside it,
all of stone, and there the bees deposit their honey.
And therein also are looms that are made of stone, very long,
    where
the nymphs weave their sea-purple webs, a wonder to look on;
and there is water forever flowing. It has two entrances,
one of them facing the North Wind, where people can enter,
but the one toward the South Wind has more divinity. That is
the way of the immortals, and no men enter by that way.*[1]

ODYSSEY, XIII.102–12

But the pyre of dead Patroklos would not light. Then swift-footed
brilliant Achilleus thought of one more thing that he must do.
He stood apart from the pyre and made his prayer to the two
* winds*
Boreas and Zephyros, north wind and west, and promised them
* splendid*
offerings, and much outpouring from a golden goblet entreated
* them*
to come, so that the bodies might with best speed burn in the fire
and the timber burst into flame.
[. . .]
They came with a sudden blast upon the sea, and the waves rose
under the whistling wind. They came to the generous Troad
and hit the pyre, and a huge unhuman blaze rose, roaring.
Nightlong they piled the flames on the funeral pyre together
and blew with a screaming blast, and nightlong swift-footed
* Achilleus*
from a golden mixing bowl, with a two-handled goblet in his
* hand,*
drew the wine and poured it on the ground and drenched the
* ground with it,*
and called upon the soul of unhappy Patroklos.[2]

ILIAD, XXIII.192–232

6

PORPHYRY'S ON THE CAVE OF THE NYMPHS

An Exploration of Theurgic Theory with Reference to Porphyry's Reading of the Odyssey

As his name indicates, Porphyry of Tyre was born in Phoenicia. A student of Plotinus, before he met his Neoplatonic master, Porphyry first studied at the feet of Cassius Longinus, a Platonist who learned, alongside Plotinus, from Ammonius Saccas. The general consensus among scholars has been that Porphyry, similar to what is imagined of his master, eschewed theurgy in favor of a purely contemplative, dialectical ascent—although, as we saw in the case of Plotinus in regard to theurgy and ritual practice in general, the reality of the matter is not so cut and dry. Crystal Addey has argued quite well in her book *Divination and Theurgy in Neoplatonism* that not only was Porphyry likely not completely opposed to theurgy, but that "Porphyry's *Philosophy from Oracles* is a theurgic text."[1] This is an admittedly bold statement that demands some qualification. Addey's evidence for this claim is fourfold. First, she begins by noting that the overall theurgic nature of the work is suggested by the fact that Porphyry conceptualizes allegorical interpretation as necessitating ideas of initiation and secrecy.

> Oracles, which are symbols [*symbola*] that need to be decoded allegorically, are also implicitly compared and assimilated with mystery rituals, since the insight available within oracles and mystery rituals requires an 'initiation' and can only be understood by those who are initiated. [. . .] To read and understand them in the appropriate manner gives the philosopher direct, experiential understanding of [nous] (Intellect).[2]

Addey's second reason for characterizing *Philosophy from Oracles* as a theurgic text is that Porphyry insists that the oracles chosen for the work are possessed of a soteriological or salvific function since "the reception of oracles can aid the salvation of the soul." This function, Addey rightly notes, "was the central goal of theurgy."[3] Third, "many oracles and fragments from the *Philosophy of Oracles*," she says, "are concerned with ritual instruction and the means of contacting the divine realm upon humans through divination: this is one of the central tenets of theurgy and further suggests the theurgic basis of this work."[4] Finally, Addey observes that, in the *Philosophy of Oracles,* Porphyry endorses a model of "persuasive necessity" as the basis for invocations of the gods, as opposed to simple, imperative compulsion, which suggests a close parallel with the definition of theurgy provided by Iamblichus in *De mysteriis:* "theurgy works through the divine love and providence of the gods who bestow their presence upon human beings through divine illumination."[5]

Furthermore, Addey makes the radical proposition that the documents exchanged between Porphyry and Iamblichus in the forms of *Letter to Anebo* and *De mysteriis* were in fact a dynamic application of two genres of philosophy: the problems and solutions genre (a method of exegesis within Platonism) and the traditional Platonic dialogue.

> Thus, rather than viewing the debate as a hostile exchange between a skeptical Porphyry and an angry Iamblichus, I have suggested that

this dialogue might have been deliberately constructed to produce a comprehensive account of theurgy and religious phenomena—primarily for educational, protreptic and initiatory purposes [. . .] and secondly, as a defense of theurgy and religious practice against Christian polemic and criticism.[6]

Judging by her charming interview with Fontainelle, Nilüfer Akçay, the author of the book *Porphyry's* On the Cave of the Nymphs *in Its Intellectual Context,* seems to at least partly share Addey's convictions in regard to the Phoenician and theurgic ritual.[7]

Before we get into the subject of Porphyry's *On the Cave of the Nymphs,* it may be advantageous to make a few observations about the tendency among ancient philosophers to treat Odysseus as a spiritual hero or exemplar; that is, to treat him as "a symbol of the highest class of humanity—those philosophers and mystics who have reached their spiritual Home,"[8] as Uždavinys remarked in an earlier passage. We have already seen that Homer was elevated in a similar regard.

To begin with, the Pythagoreans were already considering the "song of the Sirens" as representing the "music of the spheres," the beauty of which is said to lift the soul in its theurgic ascent to the Good—assuming that, as Algis Uždavinys notes, the "ears" of those souls "are not sealed by irrational passions as those of Odysseus' companions, blocked by wax."[9] We encountered a similar idea earlier among the "technical" Hermetists. Later, by the fifth century BCE, the Cynics were beginning to interpret the character of Odysseus as an *"exemplum,* or *paradeigma"*[10] of the philosopher-sage, according to Uždavinys. Odysseus's dressing in rags toward the end of Homer's *Odyssey,* for instance, is treated by the Cynics as a model for the very life advocated by Cynicism—one of poverty, humility, and detachment. Stephen R. Hill, who published a comparative study of the *Odyssey* and the *Ramayana,* suggests that the whole of the *Odyssey* may be viewed as the story of a man who has to be stripped of everything in the process of surrendering himself, for example.

"Restless seas" are themselves a symbol of the troubles of man in the iron age, and in one sense Odysseus' journey is to a life beyond the restless seas. Having arrived at Skheria, Odysseus proceeds to outline to his hosts the seven years of his great wanderings that have preceded his arrival on Kalypso's island. During these wanderings Odysseus has had to face twelve major obstacles, which are in fact spiritual tests of his developing powers. At the outset he is surrounded by many companions but they are *nepioi,* meaning "foolish," and they are gradually lost or killed, until Odysseus alone returns to Ithaka.[11]

Odysseus had to learn to surrender before he could be reunited with his real creative power, represented by Odysseus's wife, Penelope. Along similar lines, Swiss metaphysician Titus Burckhardt follows Porphyry in his interpretation of Penelope as the "soul in its original purity, as the faithful wife of the spirit." According to Burckhardt,

> [e]very path leading towards spiritual realization requires of man that he strip himself of his ordinary and habitual ego in order that he may truly become 'himself,' a transformation which does not take place without the sacrifice of apparent riches and of vain pretensions, and thus not without humiliation.[12]

Uždavinys's comments echo Burckhardt's perceptive sentiments: "Odysseus' homecoming is the journey of the initiate, which involves various tests, encounters with divine powers, transformations and return to the paternal *Nous.*"[13] In the *Life of Homer,* attributed to Pseudo-Herodotus but likely belonging to the second century after Christ,[14] the author often makes the claim that Homer "hints at" (*ainittetai*) the various doctrines of later philosophers, such as Pythagoras and Plato. For example, metensomatosis—the migration into one body of different souls—is presented in the *Life of Homer* as a legitimate Pythagorean doctrine that "was not beyond the understanding of Homer." Classical scholar Richard Lamberton notes the following about Homer's view of metensomatosis:

The talking horses of Achilles and the old dog that recognizes Odysseus indicate that the souls of men and other animals are related, and the destruction of Odysseus's crew as punishment for killing the sacred cattle is viewed as a general indication that all animals are honored by the gods [. . .]. The subsequent passage [. . .] on Circe as the symbol of the cycle of metensomatosis, to which the "thinking man" [. . .] Odysseus is immune, already suggesting something more sophisticated.[15]

As to which "subsequent passage" Porphyry refers, we shall see below. A fragment from an unknown work, preserved in the Stobaeus fragments, has Porphyry, while foreshadowing (or echoing) something of the penetrating analysis presented in *On the Cave of the Nymphs,* reiterating Plutarch's vindications. Here follows the revealing fragment in full, from Lamberton's book *Homer the Theologian.*[16]

What Homer says about Circe contains an amazing view of things that concern the soul. He says:

> *Their heads and voices, their bristles and their bodies*
> *were those of pigs, but their minds were solid, as before.*
> [*Od.* 10.239–40]

Clearly, this myth is a riddle concealing what Pythagoras and Plato have said about the soul: that it is indestructible by nature and eternal, but not immune to experience and change and that it undergoes change and transfer into other types of bodies when it goes through what we call "destruction" or "death." It then seeks out, in the pursuit of pleasure, that which is fitting and appropriate to it because it is similar and its way of life is similar in character. At this point, by virtue of what each of us gains through education and philosophy, the soul, resembling the good and repelled by shameful and illicit pleasures, is able to prevail and watch itself carefully and take care lest through inattention it be reborn as a beast and fall in love with a body badly suited for virtue and impure, nurturing an uncultivated and irrational nature and encouraging the appetitive and passionate elements of the soul rather than the rational. Empedocles calls the fate and nature that preside over this transformation a [daimon] and giving them new clothes.

> *Wrapping souls in an alien tunic of flesh,*
> *and giving them new clothes.*
>
> [FR. B126 (D–K)]

Homer, for his part, calls the cyclical progress and rotation of metensomatosis "Circe," making her a child of the sun, which is constantly linking destruction with birth and back again with destruction and stringing them together. The island of Aiaia is both the fate that awaits the dead and a place in the upper air. When they have first fallen into it, the souls wander about disoriented and wail and do not know where the west is.

> *Or where the sun that lights mortal men goes beneath*
> *the earth.*
>
> [*OD.* 10.191]

The urge for pleasure makes them long for their accustomed way of life in and through the flesh, and so they fall back into the witch's brew of [genesis], which truly mixes and brews together the immortal and the mortal, the rational and the emotional, the Olympian and the terrestrial. The souls are bewitched and softened by the pleasures that lead them back again into [genesis], and at this point they have special need of great good fortune and self-restraint lest they follow and give in to their worst parts and emotions and take on an accursed and beastly life.

The "meeting of three roads"* that is imagined as being among the shades in Hades is actually in this world, in the three divisions of the soul, the rational, the passionate, and the appetitive. Each path or division starts from the same source but leads to a life of a specific sort appropriate to it. We are no longer talking about a myth or a poem but about truth and a description of things as they are. The claim is that those who are taken over and dominated by the appetitive part of the soul, blossoming forth at the moment of transformation and rebirth, enter the bodies of asses and animals of that sort that lead turbulent lives made impure by love of pleasure and gluttony. When a soul that has had its passionate part made completely savage by hardening contentiousness and murderous brutality stemming from some disagreement or enmity comes to its second birth, gloomy and full of fresh bitterness, it casts itself into the body of a wolf or a lion, projecting as it were this body as a defense for its ruling passion and fitting itself to it. Therefore where death is concerned, purity is just as important as in an initiation, and you must keep all base emotion from the soul, put all painful desire to sleep, and keep as far from the mind as possible all jealousy, ill will, and anger, as you leave the body.

---

*The reference to a "meeting of three roads" immediately reminds us of Hecate and the Parmenides poem. But we are also reminded of the poem "The Pythagorean Y," attributed to Maximinus, which reads (quoted from Guthrie, *The Pythagorean Sourcebook and Library*, 158):

> *The Pythagoric letter two ways spread,*
> *Shows the two paths in which Man's life is led.*
> *The right hand track to sacred Virtue tends,*
> *Though steep and rough at first, in rest it ends;*
> *The other broad and smooth, but from its Crown*
> *On rocks the Traveller is tumbled down.*
> *He who to Virtue by harsh toil aspires,*
> *Subduing pains, worth and renown acquires:*
> *But who seeks slothful luxury, and flies,*
> *The labor of great acts, dishonor'd dies.*

Hermes with his golden staff—in reality, reason [logos]—meets the soul and clearly points the way to the good. He either bars the soul's way and prevents its reaching the witch's brew or, if it drinks, watches over it and keeps it as long as possible in a human form.

Porphyry's analysis in the above unnamed fragment is very much in agreement with that presented by the author of the *Life of Homer.* Proclus says similarly in his commentary on *Euclid's Elements* that:

> [the very act of] understanding would be the highest goal of the dis-
> cipline of geometry, truly performing the task of Hermes' gift, liber-
> ating the understanding from a Calypso and leading it upward to a
> more perfect and more noetic knowledge, freeing it from the partial
> perceptions of imagining.[17]

And, in his commentary on Plato's *Parmenides,* the Lycian writes:

> Many are the wanderings and circlings of the soul: one among imag-
> inings, one in opinions and one before these in understanding. But
> only the life according to [nous] has stability and this is the mysti-
> cal harbor of the soul to which, on the one hand, the poem leads
> Odysseus through the great wanderings of his life, and to which we
> too shall draw ourselves up, if we would reach salvation.[18]

Significantly for our purposes, in the *Life of Homer,* Odysseus's *nekyia* (a rite in which ghosts are called up and questioned about the future) is viewed as an example of "separating [the] soul from [the] body."[19] In fact, Martin Bernal, British scholar of modern Chinese political history, went so far as to maintain that the *Odyssey* is in reality a Greek version of the *Egyptian Book of Coming Forth by Day,* better known as the *Egyptian Book of the Dead.*[20]

Moreover, Odysseus didn't just have control over the actions of his own soul. As the earliest recorded Greek necromancer, Homer tells us that he also held sway over the souls of others—namely, of the deceased, whom Odysseus had the power to conjure. Goetic magician Jake Stratton-Kent writes:

> Odysseus as necromancer, like all necromancers, is a seeker after knowledge. His motive is to discover how to return to his homeland and family, overcoming the enmity of the sea-god Poseidon; his divination by the dead is required to accomplish this. [. . .] The ritual Odysseus performs according to Circe's instructions, which is mirrored in known Greek ritual, involves digging a trench the length and width of a man's arm. Odysseus moves around this trench pouring offerings to the dead. These consist of a mixture of honey and milk, followed by sweet wine, and lastly water. Over these is sprinkled white barley, after which the spoken evocation of the dead is made. A promise is then made to the dead that, upon his safe arrival home, a barren heifer will be sacrificed to the dead. The pyre for the burnt offering is to include a mass of precious materials, and there is to be a separate sacrifice of a fine black ewe for Tiresias.[21]

Odysseus then proceeds with the animal sacrifice. *Odyssey* XI.34–37 reads:

> *Now when, with sacrifices and prayers, I had so entreated*
> *the hordes of the dead, I took the sheep and cut their throats*
> *over the pit, and the dark-clouding blood ran in, and the souls*
> *of the perished dead gathered to the place, up out of Erebos.*[22]

Immediately after Odysseus had slain the animals, the souls of the dead proceeded to rise up from Hades, "swarming"—thereby reminding us of the line from Sophocles, which Porphyry quotes in his Homeric commentary:

> *In swarms while wandering, from the dead,*
> *A humming sound is heard.*[23]

Stratton-Kent resumes his exquisite explication:

> Odysseus now, following the advice of Circe, brandishes his sword over the blood to keep the ghosts from it until Tiresias has appeared and spoken to him. [. . .] At this stage there is a task for the men who follow Odysseus. [. . .] They are to flay and prepare the bodies of the sacrificed animals for the pyre, make the burnt offering and pray to (invoke) Hades and Persephone. Odysseus meanwhile stays seated and motionless; with his sword in his hand preventing the dead from approaching the blood until Tiresias appears and speaks to him. When Tiresias arrives and recognises him he bids Odysseus step back from the trench, withdrawing his sword, so that he may approach the blood.[24]

In regard to Odysseus's own soul, Lamberton writes that "there exists in Middle Platonism a developed allegory of Odysseus as rational man passing through the created sublunary universe (*genesis*) and returning to his celestial home."[25] Thus does Numenius of Apamea see Odysseus as escaping *genesis,* the realm of "becoming," symbolized by the waters of Poseidon. Numenius's analysis immediately reminds us of Teiresias's enigmatic words to Odysseus concerning the completion of his long ordeal: when Odysseus arrives at a place so divorced from water and thus from material generation that the airy, pneumatic inhabitants there mistake his boat oar for a winnowing fan, he will have arrived "home."

> The end of Odysseus' journey over the dark and stormy sea of generation would be marked by complete ignorance of material [i.e., *marine*] works: when a wayfarer, seeing Odysseus' oar, would think that it was a winnowing fan, then the ultimate surrender and return to the divine Intellect would be accomplished.[26]

"[U]ntil you reach those who know not the sea," Teiresias warns, where there are, "[men] eating food not mixed with [sea] salt."[27] Interestingly, according to Uždavinys, the Byzantine commentators of Homer believed that line 296 of Book XIII, which concerns Odysseus's retelling of Teiresias's prophecy regarding the "winnowing fan" to Penelope, was the final line of the *Odyssey*.[28]

In short, like Homer who authored him, Odysseus has long been seen by a number of philosophers to be a spiritual exemplar and divine revelator, disclosing something of the intelligible realm (to which Homer was believed by many to be privy) to sensible readers of the *Iliad* and *Odyssey* for centuries. Impressively, Pseudo-Herodotus indicates that, taken together, Homer's *Iliad* and *Odyssey* are nothing shy of "a vast encyclopedia with a complex, sometimes obscure, structure of meaning."[29] It is within this tradition of allegorical interpretation that we locate Porphyry's probing text.

In advance of discussing *On the Cave of the Nymphs,* we also need to say a thing or two in regard to a couple of other philosophers about whom very little is known but that bridge the gap between the Middle Platonists and the Neoplatonists—Cronius the Pythagorean and Numenius of Apamea—from whom Porphyry borrowed liberally in his Homeric commentary.

Porphyry tells us that Cronius had a penchant for philosophically explicating the Homeric epics—a task that Stobaeus says he "accomplished [. . .] most ably."[30] And he is said to have authored at least one book on the subject of reincarnation. John Dillon notes that:

> Cronius' only named work is one *On Reincarnation* (mentioned by Nemesius of Emesa, *Nat. Hom.* P. 116, 3ff. Matthei), in which he apparently denied metempsychosis into animals, but he is quoted by Porphyry, along with Numenius, as an exegete of the *Cave of the Nymphs,* and by Proclus as commenting on at least the Nuptial Chamber (*In Remp.* II22.20ff Kroll) and the Myth of Er (*In Remp.* II.109.7ff) of the *Republic*.[31]

Uždavinys informs us too that Cronius also thought that Er was a real, historical person who had actually been teacher to none other than the Iranian prophet Zoroaster.[33] The reader will recall that, along with

Zostrianos, Nicotheus, Allogenes, and *Messus, Zoroaster* was the title of a Gnostic treatise in circulation in Plotinus's school.

Numenius, on the other hand, is known to have authored no fewer than twelve books—all of which are lost, save sixty scant fragments. Remarkably, six of Numenius's twelve were the various volumes of a Platonic work titled *On the Good*—a book that Dillon, judging from the remaining fragments, thought more resembled a dialogue found in the Hermetica than a Platonic dialogue.[34] As we've already seen in chapter 5, there are similarities in the structure of Plato's dialogues and those recorded in the *Corpus Hermeticum.* Other titles by Numenius included *On the Academics' Betrayal of Plato;* the possibly Orphic *On the Indestructability of the Soul;* the Pythagorean-sounding *On Number, On Place;* the provocative *On Plato's Esoterica;* and a work called *Epops.* This last title is interesting in that, while an *epop* is a type of bird—the hoopoe bird,* specifically—Numenius likely uses it here as a play on the word *epopt,* "seer," a title that was applied to adepts of the greater mystery celebrated at the Telesterion in Eleusis. This is not too surprising as Proclus, who considered Numenius a leading Platonist, said that the man from Apamea was in the habit of "stitching the Platonic sayings to astrological lore and this to the teachings of the [Eleusinian] Mysteries."[34] For instance, the Roman philosopher Macrobius (ca. 400 CE) writes in his commentary on Cicero's *Dream of Scipio:*

> Again, dreams disclosed the displeasures of the divinities to Numenius (who among philosophers is rather curious about occult matters), because while interpreting the Eleusinian rites he made them public; it seemed to him that he saw the Eleusinian goddesses themselves, standing in harlots' clothing before an open brothel. And when he marveled at this and demanded the reasons for a dis-

---

*In Jewish lore, the hoopoe bird was entrusted with the task of guarding within its nest the mysterious *shamir,* a weird worm that had the power to cut through stone and was used to shape rough ashlars, or unworked stones. The ashlars, thus perfected, would then be used to construct King Solomon's temple.

grace not befitting divinity, they responded in anger that they had been violently dragged away from the sanctuary of their chastity and had been prostituted to all comers by Numenius himself.[35]

Proclus also says that Numenius wrote a commentary on the "Myth of Er"—a legend that we covered in chapter 2 and that influenced Numenius's (and Porphyry's) reading of *Odyssey,* XIII.102–12.

Significantly for us, Numenius's theology is closely related to that of the *Chaldæan Oracles,* which he actually references. Fragment 7 of the *Oracles* reads:

For the Father perfected all things and handed them over to the Second Intellect, which you—the entire human race—call the First Intellect.[36]

Compare to fragment 17 from Numenius:

O men, the one which you surmise to be Intellect is not the First, rather there is another Intellect before this one which is more august and more divine.[37]

Fascinatingly, Numenius does not attribute the above allusion to the *Chaldæan Oracles* or even the Juliani but rather to Plato himself. The implication may be that Numenius was not only aware of the tradition attributing the dictation of the *Oracles* to the soul of Plato, but that he also embraced it. In any case, what is left of Numenius's writings is so fragmentary that it is impossible to say with any certainty what exactly is meant. But what we can say is that Numenius's work made an enormous impact on the thinking and writings of Porphyry of Tyre.

In his *On the Cave of the Nymphs,* Porphyry outlines the general theory underlying the art of theurgy. As the title suggests, the scene that Porphyry treats of in his Homeric commentary concerns a mysterious cavern filled with stone kraters and amphorae (two-handled drinking vessels) in the port of Phorcys. It was there that Odysseus found himself upon his final return home to Ithaca. Here is the pertinent excerpt from the *Odyssey* in full.

> *At the head of the harbor, there is an olive tree with spreading*
> *leaves, and nearby is a cave that is shaded, and pleasant,*
> *and sacred to the nymphs who are called the Nymphs of the*
> *Wellsprings,*
> *Naiads. There are mixing bowls and handled jars inside it,*
> *all of stone, and there the bees deposit their honey.*
> *And therein also are looms that are made of stone, very long,*
> *where*
> *the nymphs weave their sea-purple webs, a wonder to look on;*
> *and there is water forever flowing. It has two entrances,*
> *one of them facing the North Wind, where people can enter,*
> *but the one toward the South Wind has more divinity. That is*
> *the way of the immortals, and no men enter by that way.*[38]

While Porphyry's entire commentary is indeed instructive, the sections that will occupy our attention here are primarily those numbered six, seven, and nine through thirteen in the Thomas Taylor translation,* although, where pertinent, we shall briefly touch upon the contents of the other sections as well. A more recent translation was published by Lamberton in 1983; however, we have opted instead to rely upon the translation of Taylor, whose nuanced magniloquence is simply unmatched in other translators.

It is notable that, in what fragments remain of his lost work *On the Styx*, Porphyry had already stated his belief that Homer expressed himself *sotto forma di enigmi*—that is, the Phoenician believed that the poet wrote in the form of enigmas or puzzles.[39] Another fragment from *On the Styx* adds in agreement:

---

*Since Thomas Taylor followed the eighteenth-century fashion of changing the names of Hellenic gods into those of the Roman, Algis Uždavinys has been obliged to restore the original Greek spelling, for example, Zeus instead of Jupiter, Odysseus instead of Ulysses, and so on (Uždavinys, *The Heart of Plotinus: The Essential Enneads,* 236).

The poet's thought is not, as one might think, easily grasped, for all the ancients expressed matters concerning the gods and [daimones] through riddles, but Homer went to even greater lengths to keep those things hidden and refrained from speaking of them directly but rather used those things he did say to reveal other things beyond their obvious meanings.[40]

We're about to find out what some of those "other things" encoded in Homer's works may have been.

In section one of *On the Cave of the Nymphs,* using Cronius as his source, Porphyry shows that, while Odysseus's Ithacensian cave truly may have existed—indeed, the Phoenician located a passage in the geographer Artemidorus of Ephesus that attests to the cave's historical reality[41]—its symbolism nonetheless remains the same, as though it were an allegorical device. For Porphyry imagines that the intentions of the Naiadic cult that originally worshipped in and thus fashioned the archaic cave, long before the Homeric epics were written down, were in agreement with his own theurgic reading of the text. Further, as has been noted, theurgy is a veritable reversal of the soul's emergence or ontology. Ergo, it makes perfect sense that Porphyry has rendered the cave not only a symbol of the created cosmos, but also of the moist and cavernous womb, dark and covering, where a garment-like body is stitched about the soul, woven around it in pulsating, blood-vessel-like "sea-purple webs" of innately intelligent life, for "the purple webs will evidently be the flesh which is woven from the blood," Porphyry purports, and "purple woolen garments are tinged from blood."[42]

In sections six and seven, Porphyry breaches the topic of the cave's honeycomb-filled stone amphorae, wherein "Homer says the bees deposit their honey." "Why," the Phoenician asks, "are the *amphorae* said not to be filled with water, but with honey-combs?" Because what Porphyry says here will come to have direct bearing on our next chapter, a close reading of the following points is absolutely imperative.

Theologists [. . .] have made honey subservient to many and different symbols, because it consists of many powers; since it is both cathartic and preservative. Hence, through honey, bodies are preserved from putrefaction, and inveterate ulcers are purified. [. . .] When, therefore, those who are initiated in the Leontic sacred rites, pour honey instead of water on their hands; they are ordered [by the initiator] to have their hands pure from every thing productive of molestation, and from every thing noxious and detestable. Other initiators [into these same mysteries] employ fire, which is of a cathartic nature, as an appropriate purification. And they likewise purify the tongue from all the defilement of evil with honey. [. . .] But the sweetness of honey signifies, with theologists, the same thing as the pleasure arising from copulation [. . .] therefore, honey is assumed in purgations, and as an antidote to putrefaction, and is indicative of the pleasure which draws souls downward to generation.[43]

We will return to these honey-filled amphorae in chapter 7.

Evoking Plato's "Allegory of the Cave" as an appropriate comparandum to Odysseus's cave, Porphyry then proceeds to turn his attention to the clever Homeric commentaries of Numenius of Apamea. In terms of the importance of Numenius's unique analysis, what little remains of his fascinating work would essentially go on to help lay the theoretical foundations of theurgy for the Neoplatonists of late antiquity. In fact, the real meat of Porphyry's reading relies almost completely upon Numenius's clever chain of clues.

Section nine of Porphyry of Tyre's *On the Cave of the Nymphs* reads:

9. With respect [. . .] to this Ithacensian cave, Homer was not satisfied with saying that it had two gates, but adds, that one of the gates was turned towards the north, but the other, which was more divine, to the south. He also says, that the northern gate was pervious to descent, but does not indicate whether this was also the case with the southern gate. For of this, he only says, "It is inaccessible to men, but it is the path of the immortals."[44]

Already, these two entrances to Odysseus's cave sound a lot like a stripped-down version of the "two adjacent openings in the earth, and opposite and above them two others in the heavens" from Plato's "Myth of Er." "The just," the reader will recall, "go upwards into the heavens through the door on the right" in the *Republic,* and "the unjust to travel downward through the opening on the left." Porphyry then proceeds to elaborate on the mystery of these two galactic "gates."

> 10. Numenius and his familiar Cronius assert, there are two extremities in the heavens, viz., the winter tropic, than which nothing is more southern, and the summer tropic, than which nothing is more northern. But the summer tropic is in Cancer, and the winter tropic in Capricorn. And since Cancer is nearest to us, it is very properly attributed to the Moon, which is the nearest of all the heavenly bodies to the earth. But as the southern pole, by its great distance, is invisible to us, hence Capricorn is attributed to Kronos (Saturn), the highest and most remote of all the planets. Again, the signs from Cancer to Capricorn are situated in the following order: and the first of these is Leo, which is the house of Helios (the Sun); afterwards Virgo, which is the house of Hermes (Mercury); Libra, the house of Aphrodite (Venus); Scorpius, of Ares (Mars); Sagittarius, of Zeus (Jupiter); and Capricornus, of Kronos (Saturn). But from Capricorn in an inverse order, Aquarius is attributed to Kronos; Pisces, to Zeus; Aries, to Ares; Taurus, to Aphrodite; Gemini, to Hermes; and in the last place Cancer to the Selene (the Moon).[45]

What Porphyry has outlined here, per Numenius and "his familiar," Cronius, is nothing shy of the theoretical framework underlying both the path of the soul upon descent into incarnation and the path of the soul upon theurgic ascent into the Ogdoad and beyond. As we'll learn in section thirteen of Porphyry's analysis, according to Pythagoras and even the ancient Egyptians, prior to incarnation, all souls orbit the heavens within the confines of the Milky Way galaxy, which, Macrobius tells us, encircles the zodiac in such a way that it intersects it where the two tropical signs—Capricorn and Cancer—are displayed. These the natural philosophers have named the "gates of the sun." [. . .] It is through these gates that the souls are believed to pass from heaven to earth, and from earth into heaven once again.[46]

"Therefore one [gate] is called that of men," Macrobius adds in reference to Plato's "Myth of Er," "the other that of gods." By "gates of the sun," Macrobius alludes specifically to a line from Book XXIV of the *Odyssey*:

They went along [. . .] and passed the gates of Helios the Sun, and the country of dreams, and presently arrived in [. . .] the dwelling place of souls, images of dead men.[47]

Intersecting the zodiac wheel at the points of Cancer and Capricorn, souls circling the Milky Way are said to enter a round of incarnation by the gate of Luna—Cancer—which the moon rules. The incarnating souls then descend successively through the gates Sol (Leo), Mercury (Virgo), Venus (Libra), Mars (Scorpio), and Jupiter (Sagittarius) before exiting the gate of Saturn (Capricorn), at which point they find themselves incarnated in newly conceived flesh-and-blood fetuses.

Pythagoras thought that the empire of Pluto began downwards from the milky way, because souls falling from thence appear to have already receded from the Gods. Hence he asserts that the nutriment of milk is first offered to infants, because their first motion commences from the galaxy, when they begin to fall into torrene bodies. On this account, since those who are about to descend are yet in Cancer, and have not left the milky way, they rank in the order of the Gods. But when, by falling, they arrive at the *Lion* [Leo], in this constellation they enter on the exordium of their future condition. And because, in the *Lion,* the rudiments of birth, and certain primary exercises of human nature, commence.[48]

This notion, that souls circled the Milky Way before and after incarnation(s), using the two intersections in the zodiac wheel as a pair of celestial gates, can be traced at least as far back as the Pyramid Texts (ca. 2300 BCE) in Sixth Dynasty Egypt, but demonstrably persists through the Coffin Texts (ca. 2000 BCE) and the *Papyrus of Ani* (ca. 1500 BCE), right up to the time of Ptolemy and Roman Egypt (ca. 30 BCE).

> The sky's door has been opened for you, the starry sky's door has been pulled open for you.
> —SPELL 228, PYRAMID TEXTS (TETI)

> The doors of the sky are opened for you by Re . . . the doors of the firmament are thrown open for you by your mother Nut.
> —SPELL 24, COFFIN TEXTS

> The Milky Way will not reject me, the rebels will not have power over me, I shall not be turned away from your portals, the doors shall not be closed against me
> —SPELL 72, PAPYRUS OF ANI[49]

"By the Roman era," explains Latura Beke, "this Egyptian view was widely accepted, and the Milky Way was seen as the abode of the gods (Ovid, Capella) and the reward of valorous and virtuous souls (Cicero, Manilius)."[50]

One thing that Macrobius mentions at this point in connection with the soul's descent, which Porphyry does not, is that after entering Cancer and prior to arriving at Leo, where "the rudiments of birth, and certain primary exercises of human nature" commence, the soul must first pass through the constellation called the Bowl of Bacchus, also known as the Crater, where, "for the first time intoxication overtakes descending souls with the influx of matter," Macrobius writes in *Comentarii in Somnium Scipionis,* "whence the companion of intoxication, forgetfulness, also begins to steal quietly upon souls at that point."[51]

When the soul is being drawn towards a body in this first protraction of itself it begins to experience a tumultuous influx of matter rushing upon it. This is what Plato alludes to when he speaks in the *Phaedo* of a soul suddenly staggering as if drunk as it is being drawn into the body; he wishes to imply the recent draught of onrushing matter by which the soul, defiled and weighted down, is pressed earthwards. Another clue to this secret is the location of the constellation of the Bowl of Bacchus, in the region between Cancer and Leo, indicating that there for the first time intoxication overtakes descending souls with the influx of matter; whence the companion of intoxication, forgetfulness, also begins to steal quietly upon souls at that point.[52]

As the reader may have gathered, the constellation called the Bowl of Bacchus by Macrobius is one and the same as Apollo's mythical cup, which, as we saw in chapter 1, the Olympian angrily thrust into the sky—along with a certain disobedient raven and an innocent water snake. Unlike the cup of "mind" we encountered in the *Corpus Hermeticum,* which was filled with nous and thus arguably related to the Platonic concept of *anamnesis* or divine remembering, when the soul is baptized in Apollo's Crater, it acquires the very lapse of memory that anamnesis is understood to correct. Here, one cannot help but be reminded of the enigmatic references to Lēthē, the river of forgetfulness, in the so-called Orphic golden tablets, covered in chapter 1 in connection to katabasis and the Presocratic philosophers. Macrobius resumes:

> Now if souls were to bring with them to their bodies a memory of the divine order of which they were conscious in the sky, there would be no disagreement among men in regard to divinity; but, indeed, all of them in their descent drink of forgetfulness, some more, some less. Consequently, although the truth is not evident to all on earth, all nevertheless have an opinion, since opinion is born of failure of the memory. Truth is more accessible to those who drank less of forgetfulness because they more easily recall what they previously knew above.[53]

Notwithstanding, there is one glaring discrepancy, which the perceptive reader has doubtless already identified: the Crater is clearly not located on the cusp of Cancer and Leo, just after the lunar "portal of the sun." As we stated in chapter 1, the Bowl of Bacchus or the Crater is found between the signs of Virgo and Libra, in close proximity to its sister constellations Hydra and Corvus. Nevertheless, the late William Harris Stahl, historian of ancient science, helpfully elucidates:

Actually the constellation [Crater] is located between Corvus and Hydra. Cf. Aratus *Phaenomena* 448. But if during the evening in the spring the observer faces south and looks almost overhead, he will see how the souls, passing through the descending portal of Cancer, by veering slightly to the left, would go by Crater.[54]

This, dear reader, is the reason why Porphyry went to such great lengths to emphasize the fact that Homer seemed to highlight the curious craters located inside the Cave of the Nymphs. Based on the constellation's association with the "portal of the sun," one might even go so far as to say that the crater(s) in Odysseus's cave are, in all probability, placed near the entrance that is "facing the North Wind," as the poet says, "where people [as opposed to 'immortals'] can enter."[55]

On the other hand, rather than retracing the soul's steps and going back the way she came, according to Porphyry, the path of the soul after death—and, not coincidentally, the path of theurgic ascent—follows the opposing curve of the zodiac wheel, climbing each successive sign, from Capricorn back to Cancer. Entering the gate of Saturn, the ascending soul then meets a second Saturnal gate (Aquarius) before climbing consecutively through the gates of Jupiter (Sagittarius), Mars (Aries), Venus (Taurus), and Mercury (Gemini). The soul finally exits the round of incarnation via the gate of Luna, through which she had initially descended in the first place. Significantly, rather than birth, Macrobius associates this half of the cycle with funeral rites.

Aquarius is opposite to the Lion, and presently sets after the Lion rises; hence, when the sun is in Aquarius, funeral rites are preformed to departed souls, because he is then carried in a sign which is contrary or adverse to human life.[56]

It is in fact in the context of a funeral rite that Proclus reveals the ritualistic method of theurgic ascent in his commentary on Plato's *Republic*. We will learn more about that in chapter 7.

Importantly, an identical model of soul ascent was apparently in use among a contemporaneous group of Gnostics, a sect that April D. DeConick, a professor of Near Eastern studies and early Christianity, has referred to as the "*Ophian-Christians*,"[57] which helps to illustrate just how in practice such an ascent of the soul might have looked. The second-century philosopher Celsus penned an attack against the early Christians titled *The True Word*. In it, he purported to divulge the secret rituals of the early Christian community, which involved a complicated ceremony of initiation, referred to as "The Seal."[58] Father Alexander Schmemann, the dean of Saint Vladimir's Orthodox Theological Seminary from 1962 until his death in 1983, tells us in his book on baptism and chrismation* in the Eastern Orthodox Church that:

> after the baptismal immersion and the vesting in the white garment, the neophyte is *anointed* or, to use the language of the liturgy, *sealed* with the Holy Chrism. [It is] "[the] seal of the gift of the Holy Spirit." [. . .] Such is the meaning of this ineffable mystery, of the *seal*. In the early Church the term *sphragis* (seal) [referred to] the *seal* that [. . .] is the *sign* of our high and unique calling.[59]

Thus does the neophyte, referred to in the ceremony recorded by Celsus as "Youth" and "Son," say to his "Father" initiator: "I have been anointed

---

*A sacrament in Eastern Christianity that is the equivalent of confirmation in the Roman Catholic Church.

with a white oil from the tree of life." According to Origen, in his voluminous rebuttal to Celsus's accusations, the individuals responsible for anointing the neophytes with this "white oil from the tree of life" had claimed to him that, during the rite, "there are seven angels standing on each side of the body as the soul leaves it."[60] Therefore, like Aristaeus of Proconnesus, Hermontimus of Clazomenae, and the later theurgists, this early group of Ophian-Christians were preoccupied with the liberation of the volatile soul from its bodily container.

It also must be mentioned that the motif of bodily anointment and soul ascent resembles nothing so much as the use of the so-called witches' ointments or flying unguents from medieval times, with which the witches were said to make their night flights to the witches' sabbath. In fact, just like the witches who were accused of transforming into various animal shapes, according to Celsus, "when the practitioners 'go up into' [. . .] the archontic realms, some of them become lions, some bulls, and others serpents or eagles or bears or dogs."[61] We have already seen that this is also true for the Siberian shaman during his soul flights—not to mention the therianthropy inflicted on Odysseus's men by Circe, who was a *polyphármakos,* meaning "skilled in many drugs or charms." Psychedelic historian Thomas Hatsis masterfully demonstrates in his book *The Witches' Ointment: The Secret History of Psychedelic Magic* that these salves were oftentimes said to contain a number of powerful *phármaka:* hallucinogenic nightshades that are known to elicit such an out-of-body experience, including *Atropa belladonna, Mandragora officinarum,* and *Hyoscyamus niger*[62]—the latter being a plant that has also been directly linked to the subjective experience of therianthropy.[63] The Apollonian Pythia priestesses at Delphi are said to have breathed the smoke of burning *Hyoscyamus niger* (henbane) seeds to provide them with oracular visions as well.[64] Brian C. Muraresku writes in his *New York Times* bestseller, *The Immortality Key: The Secret History of the Religion with No Name*:

> Pliny credited the appearance of henbane to Hecate's pet, Cerberus, from whose urine the plant first sprang from the earth. The

Greek naturalist referred to the plant as *"Herba Apollinaris"* (herb of Apollo), claiming that the Pythia priestess at Delphi inhaled the smoke of smoldering henbane seeds to produce their oracular visions. Another ancient term for the species, *Pythonion,* cements the connection.[65]

Also, we see from the Mithras Liturgy that this motif of bodily anointment and soul ascent was not unique to the Ophian-Christians in the ancient world. For example, Wouter Hanegraaff has said that:

[if] you look closely enough [at the Mithras Liturgy] then you have to conclude that the use of entheogenic substances played a rather important role in what is described there. [. . .] But the specific case of the "Mithras Liturgy" [. . .] may be considered one of the most important "trip reports" that we have from late antiquity. It describes a really spectacular visionary sequence and includes the detailed recipe for making an "eye paint" that you need to rub in or around your eyes to have such visions. It contains several components that are known to be psychoactive [including] the blue lotus, which was common in Egypt, has been analyzed and turns out to have hallucinogenic properties.[66]

It is not inconceivable, therefore, that these Ophian-Christians' "white oil from the tree of life," which incorporated one or more entheogenic ingredients, induced a sufficient feeling of discorporeality in the initiate that he believed he was actually experiencing vertical soul flight or therianthropy.

As the initiate ascends, he is to offer at each successive planetary gate a prescribed prayer to a guarding archon. According to Origen, the first prayer is addressed to an unnamed archon from whom the powers of the Ogdoad originate.

I greet the Solitary King, the bond of blindness, the reckless forgetting, the First Power, guarded by the Spirit of Pronoia and by Sophia.

Thence I am sent forth pure, already a part of the light of the Son and the Father. May Grace be with me. Yes, Father, may it be with me.[67]

The next gate is that of Ialdabaoth, which the group in question identified as Saturn. This prayer reads:

> (I greet) you, First and Seventh, born to rule with audacity, Ialdabaoth! As a ruling Logos of pure Nous, as a perfect work for the Son and the Father, by the imprint of the seal bearing the symbol of life, opening your cosmic gate that was shut forever, as a free man I go past your authority again. May Grace be with me. Yes, Father, may it be with me.[68]

To the archon of the next gate, Iao, the candidate, is to pray:

> (I greet) you, the Archon from whom the mysteries of the Son and the Father are concealed, Iao, the Second Lord Shining-in-the-Night and the first Lord of Death! As part of the Innocent One, wearing already my own beard as a symbol, (I am) prepared to go past your sovereignty, since by the Living Word I have overpowered that which was born from you. May Grace be with me. Father, may it be with me.[69]

After penetrating Iao's gate, next in turn is that of Sabaoth.

> Archon of the Fifth Power, Commander Sabaoth, Defender of the Law of your creation which is being destroyed by Grace! By a mightier Pentad, let me go past, since you see the symbol not open to attack by your craft. (I am) protected by the image of the imprint, since (your) body is destroyed by the Pentad. May Grace be with me. Yes, Father, may it be with me.[70]

Astaphaeus is the following archon, which the candidate must appease. The prayer to him is as follows.

Archon of the Third Gate, Astaphaeus, Overseer of the
First-Water-Source! Since you are looking at one who is an initiate,
let me pass. By the Virgin Spirit, (I) have been purified, perceiving
the essence of the cosmos. May Grace be with me. Yes, Father, may
it be (with me).[71]

Next in succession is the penultimate gate of Ailoaeus.

Archon of the Second Gate, Ailoaeus! Let me pass since I bring to
you your Mother's symbol, Grace that is hidden by the powers of
the Authorities. Grace be with me. Yes, Father, may it be with me.[72]

Finally, the last archon whose gate must be passed is named Horaeus.
His prayer reads:

You who mount the wall of fire without fear, the Archon who pro-
tects the First Gate, Horaeus! Let me pass, since you see the symbol
that destroys your power with the imprint of the tree of life. (Your
power has been) seized by the image according to the likeness of
Innocence. May Grace be with me. Yes, Father, may it be with me.[73]

Before we move on from the subject of Gnostic ascent, it is noteworthy
that a similar rite of *anagogē* may be found in the *Second Book of Jeu* of
the Bruce Codex, which preserves a detailed account of a strange series
of Gnostic baptismal elevations. In this case, however, there is a curious
addition: an unknown plant called *cynocephalon,* meaning "dog-headed,"
is held in the mouth by the initiate during the baptismal submersion.[74]
Strangely, Pliny the Elder records that this same *cynocephalia* has been
used in the past in a necromantic context to summon the ghost of none
other than our epic poet Homer![75]

We know from Celsus that the ritual was specifically one of ascent
through the seven planetary heavens known to the ancients. However,
as DeConick points out in her essay, the above arrangement of prayers
has been baffling scholars. Not only does the order not match that of

the Ptolemaic model that we saw in the *Corpus Hermeticum* (ascending from the moon to Saturn), but they also seem to be somewhat reversed to boot, with Saturn—the furthest planet from Earth—being the second gate encountered and Luna—the nearest "planet"—the last barrier crossed. Moreover, a prayer to Adonaeus, the archon of Sol, is missing from the set entirely. Until the correlation with Numenius's system, as outlined by Porphyry in *On the Cave of the Nymphs,* was discovered, it was largely suspected that Origen had made a complete mess of the arrangement. Little could be further from the case, however. Porphyry clearly states that the signs from Cancer to Capricorn, which constitute the descent of a soul into a body,

> are situated in the following order: and the first of these is Leo, which is the house of Helios (the Sun); afterwards Virgo, which is the house of Hermes (Mercury); Libra, the house of Aphrodite (Venus); Scorpius, of Ares (Mars); Sagittarius, of Zeus (Jupiter); and Capricornus, of Kronos (Saturn).[76]

"But from Capricorn," he adds, the ascent is naturally "in an inverse order." That is, in an inverse order on the opposing curve of the wheel of the zodiac.

> Aquarius is attributed to Kronos; Pisces, to Zeus; Aries, to Ares; Taurus, to Aphrodite; Gemini, to Hermes; and in the last place Cancer to the Selene (the Moon).[77]

Only upon the soul's descent into a body is the sun's sign (Leo) encountered. This leaves only the problem of the unnamed archon guarding the first gate. DeConick offers us some sober clarity on the matter.

> What can we make of the first prayer? Who might it have been associated with? The Archon is addressed as the "Solitary King" and the "First Power." The second prayer addresses an Archon who is both the "First" and the "Seventh" Power named Ialdabaoth. Why is he

the *First* and the *Seventh?* Because in the descent pattern, Ialdabaoth is the seventh Archon encountered. He is the Archon responsible for genesis, putting the soul into a physical body when it passes through the seventh gate in the descent journey, Capricorn. The reference to the First must correspond to the ascent pattern, where Ialdabaoth guards the Gate of Capricorn, the first gate in the journey upwards through the Zodiac. Thus he is the *First* and the *Seventh.*

If this is the case, then the unnamed Archon addressed in the first prayer, the "Solitary King" and the "First Power," must be Ialdabaoth. But isn't the second prayer addressed to Ialdabaoth too? Why would we have two prayers addressed to the same Archon? Because, in the ascent journey, Ialdabaoth also guards the gate in Aquarius, the Zodiacal sign that the initiate progresses through immediately following Capricorn. It stands to reason that we would expect the first two prayers to be addressed to Ialdabaoth, since he guards the first two gates in the ascent path through the Zodiac. This is exactly what Origen preserves for us: two prayers to the *First Power.* It also explains why, in the second prayer, the initiate tells Ialdabaoth that he is going past "your authority again."[78]

Celsus also notes that this particular mode of planetary ascent was not unknown to initiates of the cult of Mithras. This actually is not that surprising as Porphyry makes direct reference to the Mithraic mysteries no less than six times in his short commentary—with at least one indirect reference.*

According to Celsus, the Mithraists used a ladder to symbolize the various levels of heavenly ascent, with seven of the rungs representing the planetary gates and an additional eighth at the top to signify the Ogdoad. Consistent with Numenius's and Porphyry's interpretation of Homer's Naiadic cave, the Mithraic mysteries were oftentimes conducted in subterranean caverns called *Mithraea* that represented the

---

*Apropos the indirect reference: "those who are initiated in the Leontic sacred rites, pour honey instead of water on their hands"—*leo* (lion) being the fourth grade in the Mithraic rites.

created cosmos. "The benches that line the walls are meant to represent the ecliptic, the path of the sun through the Zodiac," DeConick says. "The arrangement of the diurnal and nocturnal houses of the Zodiac is clearly demarcated on the benches." Moreover, "the gates of entry and exit marked on the benches are associated with Cancer and Capricorn."

> In the Mithraeum of the Seven Spheres, the gates are specifically located at the Gemini-Cancer and the Sagittarius-[Capricorn] boundaries and identified with the summer and winter solstices.
>
> The identification of the gates with Cancer and Capricorn is also depicted on the Housesteads rockbirth, only in this case with the Cancer-Leo and the Capricorn-Aquarius boundaries.[79]

In every case, the gates of entry and exit are envisaged as existing either within the signs of Cancer and Capricorn or within the liminal locale of one of their cusps.

Porphyry continues with his commentary:

> 11. Theologists therefore assert that these two gates are Cancer and Capricorn; but Plato calls them entrances. And of these theologists say that Cancer is the gate through which souls descend, but Capricorn that through which they ascend. Cancer is indeed northern, and adapted to descent; but Capricorn is southern, and adapted to ascent. The northern parts, likewise, pertain to souls descending into generation. And the gates of the cavern which are turned to the north are rightly said to be pervious to the descent of men; but the southern gates are not the avenues of the Gods, but of souls ascending to the Gods. On this account, the poet does not say that they are the avenues of the Gods, but of immortals; this appellation being also common to our souls, which are per se, or essentially, immortal. It is said that Parmenides mentions these two gates in his treatise *On the Nature of Things*.
>
> 12. The ancients, likewise, very reasonably connected winds with souls proceeding into generation, and again separating themselves

from it, because, as some think, souls attract a spirit, and have a pneumatic essence.[80]

The Phoenician says that "souls attract a spirit, and have a pneumatic essence." Here, Porphyry quietly breaches the subject of the pneumatic ochēma. He resumes:

> But the north wind is adapted to souls falling into generation; and, on this account, the northern blasts refresh those who are dying, and when they can scarcely draw their breath. On the contrary, the southern gales dissolve life. For the north wind, indeed, from its superior coldness, congeals [as it were, the animal life], and retains it in the frigidity of terrene generation. But the south wind being hot, dissolves this life, and sends it upward to the heat of a divine nature. 13. According to Pythagoras, also, the people of dreams are the souls which are said to be collected in the galaxy, this circle being so called from the milk with which souls are nourished when they fall into generation.[81]

Aside from section six, to which we will briefly return in chapter 7, section thirteen is the final one from Porphyry's impressive work that will require some comment on our part. Having already addressed sections nine and ten, the reader should find that eleven and twelve, which are possessed of closely related content, are fairly self-explanatory.

The Phoenician finally tells us that, according to Pythagoras, the disembodied souls circulating in the Milky Way galaxy are the very same entities encountered by man during his dreams. Recall that, in Book XXIV of the *Odyssey,* Homer has Odysseus pass by the "gates of Helios the Sun, and the country of dreams" to arrive in the "dwelling place of souls, images of dead men."[82] This consistency is far from coincidental. Earlier, in Book XIX, Homer had directly associated these northern and southern gates with two mysterious gates of "horn" and "ivory," through which dreams themselves are said to issue. The poet has Penelope say to Odysseus while the latter is still in disguise as an old man:

There are two gates through which the insubstantial dreams issue.
One pair of gates is made of horn, and one of ivory.
Those of the dreams which issue through the gate of sawn ivory,
these are deceptive dreams, their message is never accomplished.
But those that come into the open through the gates of the polished
horn accomplish the truth for any mortal who sees them.[83]

In the estimation of Catalin Anghelina, a professor in the humanities department at Columbus State Community College, "[the] two sets of gates in the *Odyssey*, the gates of horn and ivory and the gates of the sun, seem to be identical."[84] As we shall see in chapter 7, it was in a dream that the soul of the deceased "unhappy Patroklos" made his pleading, spectral visitation to the mourning but sleeping "swift-footed Achilleus."

It must be acknowledged, however, before moving on from the subject of these celestial gates, that Porphyry of Tyre's (and thus Numenius's) formidable description of the created cosmos does not reflect anything observable in the objective universe. Indeed, his analysis has its origins in something called the *thema mundi,* meaning the "theme of the world," which was an ancient, theoretical teaching device—a mythical horoscope for the birth of the world that was used by Hellenistic astrologers to teach important astrological concepts such as planetary aspects and domicile rulership. For instance, we know that the thema mundi has to have been purely symbolic insofar as the placement of Mercury and Venus in relation to Sol in the chart is, to put it simply, an astronomical impossibility. Truly, in the thema mundi, Mercury is placed at fifteen degrees Virgo—thirty degrees from the sun in Leo—whereas Venus is positioned at fifteen degrees Libra—sixty degrees away from the sun. However, in reality, the angular distance for Mercury is always less than 27.8 degrees away from Sol and that of Venus is never more than 47.8. Moreover, while the Milky Way does indeed intersect the zodiac wheel at two different, definite junctures, those crossroads demonstrably are not found at the points of Cancer and Capricorn. Latura Beke explains:

Macrobius is correct in placing the heavenly gates at the intersections of the Milky Way and the Zodiac (the path of the Planets), but he incorrectly places these intersections by the constellations Capricorn and Cancer (apparently following the mislead of Numenius and Porphyry). Actually, the circle of the Milky Way cuts across the band of the Zodiac at two locations: 1) between the constellations Scorpius and Sagittarius, and 2) between Gemini and Taurus (close by Orion, another important marker). In his astrological poem *Astronomica* (c. AD 10), the Roman writer Manilius has no problem locating these intersections:

"The other circle [the Milky Way] [. . .] passing between the blazing tail of the Scorpion and the tip of the Archer's left hand and arrow [. . .] [and by] the Twins through the bottom of their sign. [. . .] Nor does it [the Zodiac] elude the sight of the eye. [. . .] The other circle [the Milky Way] is placed crosswise to it."[85]

The portals are therefore, as Latura Beke describes, expressly *not* located in Cancer and Capricorn but rather between (1) Scorpio and Sagittarius and (2) Gemini and Taurus. "To illustrate the antiquity of the 'portals of the sun' at these locations (by the constellations of Scorpius and Taurus)," adds Latura Beke, "we find in the Babylonian Epic of Gilgamesh (c. 1100 BC) a solar gate guarded by Scorpion people."[86]

This solar gate is found in Neo-Assyrian art [. . .], where scorpion-men are portrayed as "attendants of Shamash" [. . .], while the exact celestial location is given when "the scorpion man" has been identified as the constellation Scorpio.[87]

"The opposite gate of the Sun, by Taurus, is often depicted as guarded by bull-men," Latura Beke adds further, "and again, it would seem evident that these bull-men (and other mythic representations of bulls) point to the constellation Taurus, as a marker for the celestial intersection at that location."[88]

Having explored the theoretical underpinnings that provide philosophical support for theurgy as a ritual procedure, we will now turn our attention away from Porphyry's *On the Cave of the Nymphs,* looking instead to Proclus's *On the Republic*—and to the only known *mimêsis** of the secretive, ceremonial praxis that constitutes the protocols and procedures of the rite of theurgic elevation proper.

Mimêsis, meaning "to mimic," is the word Finamore uses to describe the rite of elevation, which mimics Achilles's funeral rite for Patroclus.

7

PROCLUS'S COMMENTARY ON PLATO'S REPUBLIC

A Breakdown of Theurgic Praxis with Reference to Proclus's Reading of the Iliad

Born in Constantinople in the fifth century after Christ, Proclus Lycius was a student of Olympiodorus the Elder in Alexandria, who was so impressed by the young man that he actually wanted him to marry his daughter. This, however, wasn't to be as Proclus, not satisfied with Olympiodorus's mastery, still felt he had not acquired an adequate teacher and thus departed. Upon arriving in Athens, the young philosopher studied at the feet of an aging Plutarch of Athens before finally meeting his beloved teacher, Syrianus, who would eventually concede the leadership of Plato's Academy to Proclus. In fact, Proclus so loved his master that the two would actually go on to be buried together in a twin tomb. Their joint epitaph, penned by Proclus himself, reads:

> *I Proclus, here the debt of nature paid,*
> *(My country Lycia) in the dust am laid;*

> *Great Syrianus form'd my early youth,*
> *And left me his successor in the truth.*
> *One common tomb, our earthly part contains,*
> *One place our kindred souls, —th' aetherial plains.*[1]

Although we know very little about his life, and his extant writings are few, it is to Syrianus that Proclus attributes his remarkable reading of Book XXIII of Homer's *Iliad*.

Proclus is widely considered one of the greatest and certainly one of the most prolific Neoplatonists of his era. He was also an adept in several mystery schools. While living in Athens, for instance, he famously took an extended sabbatical to the Anatolian kingdom Lydia, where he was initiated into a number of Greek and Roman mystery cults that no doubt made an impact on his writings. These include extensive commentaries on Plato's books the *Cratylus*, the *First Alcibiades*, the *Parmenides*, the *Republic*, and the *Timaeus*, as well as a commentary on the first book of Euclid's *Elements*. He also penned the highly influential theological titles *Elements of Theology* and *Platonic Theology*. In regard to this last, the German philosopher Hegel once said of the book that it was a far more mature and systematic delivery of Platonic philosophy than anything offered in Plotinus's *Enneads*.[2] But it is Proclus's commentary on Plato's *Republic* that will be of primary importance to us here—and of secondary importance, Proclus's *Platonic Theology*.

In the *Republic*, Plato has Socrates turn a critical eye toward the various myths recounted in the works of Homer and Hesiod. While admitting the necessity of myths for the moral education of the citizens and especially the youth of Athens, Socrates strongly stresses that which specific myths are allowed to be disseminated at large must be closely controlled by the tight hand of the state. And because they constituted "ugly lies"[3] about the gods, the myths of Homer and Hesiod in particular were unfit for public consumption. Robert Lamberton tells us:

> Each offensive myth mentioned is viewed in terms of its potential educational impact on the guardians. The myth of Ouranos and

Kronos will encourage the young to punish their fathers (378b), and stories of the gods fighting with one another and plotting among themselves will encourage them to believe that internal strife in a society is an acceptable state of affairs (378c–e). The only solution is to abolish all the existing myths and have new ones made up according to basic principles [. . .] set by the lawmakers. (379a–c).[4]

Xenophanes had already attacked the pair of poets a century earlier for similar reasons, saying, "Homer and Hesiod have attributed to the gods all things that are blameworthy and disgraceful for men: stealing, committing adultery, deceiving each other."[5] However, as Lamberton further points out in regard to the interpretation of such mythological poems:

[A] text is no longer considered as a normal human utterance but as a piece of scripture, an utterance of a privileged sort that, whatever the frustrations and inadequacies of the process [of interpretation], must be interrogated for the sake of the important truths it is thought to contain.

It is difficult to say whether there was ever a time when the *Iliad* and *Odyssey* were *not* viewed as possessing this potential to reveal meanings beyond the obvious. What is demonstrable, however, is that the tradition of interpretation cultivated by the Neoplatonists generated a model of the meaning of these poems—and of the structure of that meaning—that departed extraordinarily from the most obvious meaning, transforming the poems into revelations concerning the nature of the universe and the fate of souls. [They] never abandoned the idea that the meanings they found in the poems had been placed there deliberately by Homer.[6]

Heraclitus, the author of *Homeric Allegories*—an angry defense of Homer against the hasty assaults of a censoring Socrates—was decidedly more extreme in his condemnation of Plato, firmly insisting on the overall superiority of the archaic, blind poet above the comparably novel

Athenian philosopher.[7] It is in this same vein of Homeric defense that Proclus picks up his pen in Essay 6 of his commentary on the *Republic* and, in the process, paints a pretty picture of the procedures and protocols of practical theurgy. For, in Proclus's estimation, Homer's poems are in perfect harmony with the philosophy of Plato, and in defense of the epic poet, Proclus made a clear distinction between three separate varieties of verse: "inspired, didactic and mimetic."[8] It is the latter two kinds, according to Proclus, that Plato has taken issue with—the Lycian regarding Homer as the chief exemplar of the former (i.e., inspired poetry—even though mimetic and didactic forms admittedly appear throughout both the *Iliad* and the *Odyssey*). In the learned view of Proclus, this:

> tragic, monstrous and unnatural element in poetic creation provokes the audience in various ways into searching for truth. It attracts us toward secret knowledge and does not allow us to rest satisfied with superficial conceptions on account of their verisimilitude, but compels us to penetrate into the interior of myths and to explore the meaning that was hidden in myths by their authors. It forces us to survey what natures and powers they included into the meaning of the myth, indicating them to posterity by means of these symbols. Myths of this kind, therefore, arouse in talented listeners a desire for their secret message, and through their apparent absurdity they stimulate them to investigate the truth located in the inner sanctuary, while preventing the uninitiated from accessing that which is not lawful for them to touch.[9]

> Authors of myths imitate the transcendent power of the models by those things which are entirely opposite to the gods and are furthest removed from them: that which surpasses nature is represented by things contrary to nature; that which is more divine than all reason, by the irrational; that which transcends in simplicity all fragmented beauty, by things that appear as ugly and obscene. It seems likely, therefore, that they do all this in order to make us recall the transcending superiority of the gods.[10]

> The myths want to indicate [. . .] through Helen, the whole of
> that beauty that has to do with the sphere in which things come to
> be and pass away and that is the product of the demiurge. It is over
> this beauty that eternal war rages among souls, until the more intel-
> lectual are victorious over the less rational forms of life and return
> hence to the place from which they came.[11]

In *Iliad* XXIII.175–78, Achilles slays twelve Trojan prisoners of war
"with a stroke of bronze"[12] before throwing their bodies upon the
funeral pyre of Patroclus. This apparent brutality, Socrates coldly denies
in the *Republic* 391a–b, saying, "[it] is not to be believed that [Achilles]
massacred the captives on [Patroclus'] pyre,"[13] to which Proclus boldly
interjects in his commentary on Plato's *Republic* I.151.25: "Regarding
those sacrificed on the funeral pyre something must be said."[14]

> [If] it is necessary to recall [. . .] the more secret contemplation of
> these verses by [Syrianus], it must be said that the whole rite (*prag-
> mateia*) conducted by Achilles around the pyre imitates the rite of
> immortalization (*apathanatismos*) of the soul among the theurgists,
> leading up the soul of Patroclus into the transcendent life.[15]

According to Proclus, the funeral rite performed by Achilles for his ill-
fated companion mimics (*mimêsis*) those rituals executed by the theurgists for the purpose of the "immortalization [. . .] of the soul." "Achilles
the Theurgist may be an even more surprising development than Homer
the Theologian," Finamore observes in direct response to this assertion,
"but that is very nearly what Proclus (following Syrianus) suggests."[16]

In the following paragraphs of Essay 6, Proclus proceeds to propound
the particular ways in which Achilles's ritual actions at the funeral pyre
of Patroclus specifically apply to the theurgic rite of *apathanatismos* or
"soul immortalization"—"leading the soul of Patroclus into the transcendent life."[17] The ritual may therefore also be characterized as a
peculiar example of psychagogia—albeit performed upon the soul of a
living man. "Thus, Syrianus regards Achilles as the prototype of the

theurgical officiant," writes Algis Uždavinys, "and Patroclus as that of the aspirant who is to be initiated into the mysteries and his soul separated by certain 'sacred methods' (*heirais methodois*). Patroclus laid out upon the pyre resembles the initiate who has undergone a symbolic death and burial, while Achilles represents the priest or master of the initiation."[18]

The rite of theurgic elevation therefore begins with a symbolic "voluntary death"[19] and the subsequent burial of the initiate, as it says in *Iliad* XXIII.135-151.* This is no ordinary burial, however, for not only is this particular burial not done in virgin soil—nay, rather in locks of human hair—but the head of the candidate for initiation is specifically said to be left uncovered. Homer writes:

> They covered all the corpse under the locks of their hair, which they cut off and dropped on him. [. . .] And now brilliant swift-footed Achilleus [. . .] stood apart from the pyre and cut off a lock of fair hair [. . .] and gazing in deep distress out over the wine-blue water, he spoke forth: [. . .] I would give my hair into the keeping of the hero Patroklos.[20]

Uždavinys explains:

> By means of this *theourgike techne,* the soul is purified, transformed, and conducted to the divine realm. [. . .] Thereby the vindicated soul is separated from the mortal receptacle and re-united with the noetic principles. Symbolically ("in the most mystic of all initiations": *en tē mustikōtatē tōn teletōn: Proclus Plat. Theol.* IV.9, p.193, 38) this separation from the gross body is represented by burying the initiate's body with the exception of the head:
>
> The head is not buried, because the soul which abides in it does not undergo "death." This sacramental act has an additional peculiar

---

*In preparation for the burial rite, Proclus mentions both purifications with seawater and sprinklings of sulphur over a fire (Majercik, *The Chaldæan Oracles,* 37).

feature: it is the initiate who at the binding of the theurgists buries his own body.[21]

Moreover, when the world's shape is regarded as a cosmic body, this body may be imagined as "a skull deprived of the remaining bodily parts."

> It resembles a human head (or rather, the human skull resembles the universe which is an agalma created by the Demiurge), being the living creature [. . .] whose structure is isomorphic to the human structure.[22]

Now, this notion of the initiate burying his own body requires at least some comment. Aside from the fact that such an injunction does not feature in Homer—indeed, Patroclus is already deceased—we would be hard pressed to explain how one might bury himself up to his own neck. This admittedly bizarre notion is something that Uždavinys encountered in the exhaustive work of Hans Lewy, who wrote in regard to the ritual act of self-burial:

> This requirement explains the glorification of voluntary death fig-uring in one of the Chaldæan fragments: "The souls of those who have left their body violently are the purest." "Violently" here may be taken to refer to the mystic voluntary suicide, as the following passage proves: "Those who thrust out the soul and inhale (sc. The "Flames"?) are easy to loose." The choice of an emphatic expres-sion for the soul's departure from the body is meant to convey that their separation is due to an act of violence. Accordingly, the "disembodiment" of the soul is interpreted by the Chaldæans as a mystic suicide, *"ad instar voluntariae mortis"** (Apuleius referring to the mysteries of Isis), and figured by a symbolic act.[23]

---

*The line from Apuleius in full reads, "both the gates of death and the guardianship of life were in the goddess's hands, and the act of initiation was performed in the manner of voluntary death" (Apuleius, *Metamorphoses,* Books 7–11, 275).

However, Ruth Majercik has taken issue with Lewy's reading, saying that "[his] interpretation of this rite as a 'mystic, voluntary suicide' is surely wrong." "Not only is the notion of death by violence (symbolic or otherwise) not attested as a Chaldean doctrine," Majercik continues, "but the one fragment which might support such a position is clearly misread by Lewy."

> A better interpretation of this Proclean passage, then, is that of Saffrey and Westerink [. . .], who suggest that this symbolic burial could correspond to the sixth "kind" of death enumerated by Damascius [. . .], viz. the "supernatural death" or "more divine way" of the theurgists, in which the elements of the body (symbolically) "dissolve" (thus assuring that the body, in its post mortem state, will be free of demonic vengeance).[24]

In any case, the motif of self-burial does not appear in Homer, nor does the theme of leaving the head of the deceased or initiate exposed. These ideas were introduced by Lewy in his *Chaldæan Oracles and Theurgy,* following Proclus in his *Platonic Theology,* and therefore do not figure into Proclus's reading of Book XXIII of the *Iliad,* as seen in his commentary on the *Republic.*

Proclus's defense of Achilles against the charges of Socrates continues:

> [S]tanding before the pyre he is said to call upon the winds, Boreas and Zephyrus (*Il.* 23.194–5), so that the manifest vehicle (*to phainomenon ochêma*) might receive its appropriate care through their visible movement, and that which is more divine than this [vehicle] might invisibly be purified and return to its own allotted sphere (*lêxis*), drawn upwards by the airy and lunar and solar rays, as one of the gods says.[25]

Exoterically, Achilles calls upon the north and west winds so that he may ignite Patroclus's funeral pyre. Esoterically, however, the invocations of Boreas and Zephyros—these two being winds or *pneuma*—serve to cleanse both the pneumatic ochēma and the psyche or soul itself, the latter then being drawn up into "its own allotted sphere." Moreover, according to Porphyry,

> [t]he ancients, likewise, very reasonably connected winds with souls proceeding into generation, and again separating themselves from it, because, as some think, souls attract a spirit, and have a pneumatic essence. But the north wind is adapted to souls falling into generation; and, on this account, the northern blasts refresh those who are dying.[26]

It is fitting, then, that Homer should have Achilles call upon this particular pneumatic force. "According to this explanation," Uždavinys writes:

> Achilles' invocation to the winds proceeds from his intention that the subtle vehicle (ochēma) of Patroclus' soul should be cleansed and restituted to its native order, being drawn upwards.[27]

Although, it is not only the pneumatic ochēma that is concerned here, but Patroclus's (and the initiate's) very soul, as John Finamore says.

> The ritual act, which takes place at night, is performed for the sake of Patroclus' soul, not merely for the visible vehicle. That is, although what one sees is the lower vehicle and although the vehicle is certainly involved in the rite, being purified in the course of it, this is most especially a rite of the immortalization of the soul itself.[28]

In Porphyry, the north wind was referenced in opposition to the south wind, creating a dichotomy of adversity—of life and death, cold and hot, and so on. The north wind, Porphyry reasons, on account of its superior coldness, congeals life and is conducive to it, but the extreme heat of the south wind, the Phoenician believes, dissolves vitality and is inimical to survival. However, Homer does not oppose the north to south wind in the *Iliad* but rather pairs the north wind with the west. Perhaps a closer reading of the function of these invocations may be found with reference to the Orphic hymns, which contains paeans to both the north and west winds.

Not unlike the two stages of initiation practiced in the ancient mysteries, according to Proclus's and Syrianus's reading of Homer, in this funeral initiation, these winds appear to fulfill a similar twofold function of katharsis (purification) and telete (perfection). Boreas, the north wind may, for example, aid those who are sloughing off material existence in the process of ascending. The Orphic hymn to Boreas (hymn number 79) says, for instance:

> *Disperse the rebellious*
> *alliance of clouds and sleet,*
> *hurry the storm*
> *to bring fair weather*
> *everywhere.*
>
> *Brighten the face of the sky,*
> *let the sun shine upon us.*[29]

Here, the material body is a veritable cloud obscuring the light of the soul, and Boreas is the force called upon to disperse that "rebellious alliance." Zephyros, the west wind, on the other hand, is said to reach even unto the dead heroes in the Elysian Fields. Orpheus's hymn to Zephyros (hymn number 80) reads:

> *Oceanus sends you*
> *to refresh the dead heroes*
> *in the Elysian Fields.*
> *Son of Dawn,*
> *adored by harbors,*
> *ships cut smooth*

when you fill sails
with your soft breeze.[30]

Not only does Zephyros reach all the way to the Elysian Fields, but it would appear that he aids the trireme-like, disincorporated soul in sailing safely past the oceans of material (re)generation. As Proclus says: "The poet is all but proclaiming to us that Achilles' ritual was concerned with the soul of his friend, and not with the manifest vehicle alone."

Proclus proceeds with his Homeric commentary. The following passages must be read slowly and with deliberation.

> *And Achilles is said to pour libations on the pyre "for a whole night":*
> *from a golden crater, taking a double cup,*
> *calling upon the soul of poor Patroclus (Il. 23.219 and 221).*[31]

This verse is simply staggering to us. Here, Achilles pours out libations for the soul of a deceased Patroclus—and that from a "golden crater," using a "double cup" (i.e., *double-handled*), resembling an amphora. *Krateres* (plural of *krater*) and amphorae are precisely what Odysseus encountered above, filled with honeycombs, in the Cave of the Nymphs. Moreover, Achilles executes these ritual actions around a funeral pyre, that is, around a blazing fire, which Porphyry explains, in *On the Cave of the Nymphs,* "is of a cathartic nature, and an appropriate purification,"[32] along with honey, which was also considered a purificant. Fire is the hot and dry element in connection to the Naiadic amphorae and honey.* Recall that in Book XIII.102–5 of the *Odyssey,* Homer wrote:

> and nearby is a cave that is shaded, and pleasant,
>   and sacred to the nymphs who are called the Nymphs of the
> Wellsprings,
>   Naiads. There are mixing bowls and handled jars inside it.[33]

---

*Honey is in Porphyry's mind an allusion to the descent through Leo—hence "Leontic" rites of the Mithraic mysteries.

The word used for bowls in the above passage from the *Odyssey* is, of course, *krateres;* the word used for handled jars is *amphorae,* meaning "two-handled jars"—hence, the "double cup" of Achilles. We stated early on that, in the *Oracles,* the mixing bowl was understood to be the province of the anima mundi or world soul, referred to by Proclus as the "spring of souls." The individual two-handled cup that Achilles uses as a ladle, then, as we have also said, alludes to Patroclus's own, individual share of soul. This interpretation is perfectly in line with Porphyry's own reading of the pertinent passage from the *Odyssey*: "[The] bees are said to deposit their honey in bowls and amphorae," Porphyry explicates, "the bowls being a symbol of fountains [and] the amphorae are symbols of the vessels with which we draw water from fountains."[34] We also learned in chapter 1 that the "mixing bowls" in the Cave of the Nymphs are indicative of the constellation Crater, through which the descending soul must pass (where it gets drunk on matter and develops a "divine amnesia") upon passing through the lunar gate—immediately following its escape (or exile) from the orbit of the Milky Way galaxy. The honey-filled amphorae, on the other hand, are possessed of a slightly similar astrological connection. As we saw in chapter 6, in *On the Cave of the Nymphs,* the Phoenician compared these honey-filled two-handled jars to the so-called Leontic sacred rites—that is, to *leo,* the title of the fourth grade in the initiatory structure of the mysteries of Mithras.* As Porphyry tells us from his own personal experience, in the Mithraic mysteries, the officiants "pour honey instead of water on their [the initiates'] hands; they are ordered [by the initiator] to have their hands pure from everything productive of molestation, and from everything noxious and detestable. [. . .] And they likewise purify the tongue from all the defilement of evil with honey."[35] Porphyry further comments on the association of honey with pleasure and procreation. He writes that "Kronos is ensnared by Zeus through honey." Kronos, filled with honey, becomes intoxicated, falls asleep, and is bound.

---

*The Mithraic grades were as follows: *corax* (raven), *nymphus* (bridegroom), *miles* (soldier), *leo* (lion), *Perses* (Persian), *heliodromus* (sun's courier), and *pater* (father).

Kronos being bound, is castrated [. . .] the theologist obscurely sig-
nifying by this, that divine natures become through pleasure bound,
and drawn down into the realms of generation; and also that, when
dissolved in pleasure, they emit certain seminal powers.[36]

As Proclus further observes: "the sweetness of honey signifies, with theologists, the same thing as the pleasure arising from copulation [. . .]
therefore, honey is [. . .] indicative of the pleasure which draws souls
downward to generation."[37]

We encountered something identical in the *Commentary on the
Dream of Scipio*. Let us take a moment to recall what Macrobius has
already told us about the path of the soul's descent:

But when, by falling, they [i.e., souls] arrive at the *Lion* [Leo], in
this constellation they enter on the exordium of their future condition. And because, in the *Lion,* the rudiments of birth, and certain
primary exercises of human nature, commence.[38]

Just as we saw with the honey-filled amphorae in Porphyry's *On the
Cave of the Nymphs*—the same of which were "indicative of the pleasure which draws souls downward to generation"—Macrobius similarly
associates the astrological sign of Leo with "the rudiments of birth, and
certain primary exercises of human nature."

Compare once more to the pertinent lines from Book XXIII.217–19
of the *Iliad,* this time from the Richmond Lattimore translation:

Nightlong they piled the flames on the funeral pyre together
and blew with a screaming blast, and nightlong swift-footed
    Achilleus
from a golden mixing bowl, with a two-handled goblet in his hand.[39]

Here, the word used for a two-handled goblet is *amphikupellon,* the
meaning of which may be essentially identical to amphora but on a
smaller, or slimmer, scale. Achilles places two similarly handled jars—

in this case, *amphiphoreas*—filled with oil and (you guessed it) honey next to the corpse of Patroclus. Likewise, the soul of Patroclus says to a dreaming Achilles, calling to mind the twin burial of Syrianus and Proclus: "Let one single vessel, the golden two-handled urn [*amphikaluptoi*] the lady your mother gave you, hold both our ashes."[40] In referencing both "mixing bowls" and "two-handled jars" in the passages taken from the *Odyssey* and the *Iliad,* it is obvious that Proclus suspects these two excerpts are intentionally and thematically linked— a notion no doubt surprising to the metamodern reader but one with which the Neoplatonists would have been perfectly at home.

At Essay 6.153.5, Proclus finally gets to the point of Socrates's primary contention with Homer, as presented in Plato's *Republic:* Achilles's slaying of the "twelve noble sons of the great-hearted Trojans," which Homer admits Achilles did "with evil thoughts against them in his heart."

> If Achilles' care for Patroclus is of this kind, it would not be out of place to say that [the] twelve who are sacrificed at the pyre are arranged as attendants for Patroclus' soul, since Achilles knows and cares for its leading part (*to hêgemonikon*). Therefore he has chosen this number as most appropriate for those who are going to follow the leading part, and since it is dedicated to the all-encompassing processions of the gods.[41]

"Thus," says Finamore, "the whole ritual enacts the soul's theurgic death and rebirth in the intelligible realm."[42] Baltzly et al. are correct when they write that "[the] *Phaedrus* is [. . .] the ultimate source of the notion of processions, which is extended in Proclus to occur at all levels of being."[43] "The number 12 and reference to the procession of the gods [. . .] return us to [the *Phaedrus*] where Zeus and eleven other gods travel through the heavens toward the Forms."[44]

> Thus the twelve sacrificed youths are symbols of the number of intelligible-and-intellectual leader-gods that the soul will follow in its ascent to the intelligible.[45]

"The reference to the procession of the *Phaedrus* recalls the burial rite of the *Platonic Theology*," Finamore adds, "and allows us to see that the two are closely related Chaldaean rites involving the soul's recovery of its true, rational nature and its return to the intelligible."

Before we close this chapter on the Homeric roots of Proclus's theurgy, we first need to address one last verse, to which Proclus failed to give any attention. At *Iliad* Book XXIII.226, Homer writes:

> At that time when the dawn star passes across earth,
> harbinger
> of light, and after him dawn of the saffron mantle is
> scattered
> across the sea, the fire died down and the flames were over.
> The winds took their way back toward home again, crossing
> the Thracian water, and it boiled with a moaning swell as
> they crossed it.
> The son of Peleus turned aside and away from the burning
> and lay down exhausted, and sweet sleep rose upon him.[46]

The "dawn star" is, of course, the planet Venus, which the Mesopotamians—the fathers of astrology and astronomy—associated with the goddess of love and war. She was originally worshipped in Sumer and Atratta as Inanna, before being exported to the surrounding areas of Assyria, Babylon, and the Akkadian Empire, where the goddess acquired the stellar name Ishtar—meaning "Queen of Heaven." And, like the queen of heaven, Venus is a heavenly body that appears to make a number of annual descents into Kur, the Sumerian underworld and land of the dead.

Jeffrey L. Cooley, professor of theology, walks us along the bridge that connects the katabatic activities of this Mesopotamian goddess to the planet Venus, in its erratic, venereal, psychopompic wanderings.

Many scholars accept that the related Sumerian tale of *Inana's Descent to the Underworld* at least in part describes the setting of the planet Venus in the west followed by her journey through the underworld and eventual rising in the east. There is, therefore, precedents for astral aspects in the interpretation of Sumerian Inana mythology. [. . .] The planet, which is the second brightest object in the night sky, is erratic in comparison to the stars and most of the other planets due to its inferior positioning between the earth and the sun. To earthly observers, most other celestial bodies rise in the east and move across the dome of the sky until they set on the western horizon. When Venus, on the other hand, rises in the east just before sunrise, it never visibly crosses the entire sky. Each night, the interval between the planet's rising and sunrise increases because the planet's distance from the sun increases. The length of its nightly visibility increases commensurably. But the planet never really escapes from the horizon (no more than 46 degrees from the sun), at one point becoming stationary, after which the time interval between its rising and the sun's decreases, until it seems to disappear from the eastern horizon, whence it came. During this period of visibility, it can be seen nightly before sunrise for about eight months. Because it moves behind the sun (i.e. superior conjunction), it is subsequently not visible in the sky at all for around eighty days. Venus then reappears, but this time on the western horizon just after sunset. Its western movements are similar to those in the east. [. . .] This second period, which is due to Venus' passing in front of the sun (i.e. inferior conjunction) can last anywhere from three days (in the winter) or over two weeks (in the summer). Venus then rises again in the east before sunrise and the whole cycle [. . .] begins again.[47]

Inanna-Ishtar's underworld descent may therefore be an allegorical, instructive device, based at least in part on certain astronomical phenomena observable in the natural world.

Homer tells us that it was the appearance of this dawn star ascending on the horizon that signaled for Achilles the end of his theurgic funeral rite for "unhappy Patroclus." This suggests that the warrior's actions may have been based, at least in part, on the widespread notion that, with the ascent of Venus from the depths of Hades, Patroclus's soul too may have had an opportunity to rise up into the heavens. Thus, do we proclaim with Proclus Lycius:

> So let us not charge him with arrogance against both men and gods nor let us disbelieve the poem, if Achilles, being the child of a goddess and Peleus, and the student of Cheiron,* did such things.[48]

Having finished our treatment of both Porphyry's and Proclus's theurgic analysis of the pertinent sections of Homer's *Odyssey* and *Iliad,* we will now set aside discussions of what Radcliffe Edmonds has called "a 'leading up' of the individual," that is, *anagogē,* to the final topic of our present study: "the perfection or purification of mortal and material things"[49]—that is, telestikē, in the form of the mysterious practice of statue animation.

---

*Also said to have been taught by Cheiron is the necromancer and statue animator Asclepius—the son of Apollo, the god of prophecy—who raised Hippolytus's spirit from the dead at the request of Artemis, Apollo's sister.

PART III

Theurgic Telestikē

8

ANIMATED AGALMATA

*A Discussion on the Process of Statue
Animation and Its Vital Role in
Practical Theurgy*

We have seen that, for the theurgists, telestikē was a central concern. Radcliffe Edmonds defined *telestikē* as "the perfection or purification of mortal and material things." Telestikē can therefore refer to both the practice of statue animation, which we encountered in the *Chaldæan Oracles,* and to a ritual process by which the human soul is divinized. In practice, the means and the ends of these two apparently disparate rites are in fact quite similar. In contrast to the anagogic type of theurgic initiation described by Proclus in the previous chapter, being kataphatic,* telestikē is really more akin to divine possession. "The initiate," says the learned Uždavinys, "is divinized like a hieratic statue by means of sacramental rites [and] contempla-

---

*Kataphatic, as opposed to apophatic. In the former, the divine element is "brought down" into objects, spaces, times, etc. In the latter, the divine is approached with an understanding that it transcends all particulars. Anything one could say about it would be a limitation and thus wrong. Another term for apophatic is *negative theology,* but *positive theology* is not a term I've ever seen used in this context. *Kataphatic theology* is a "theology of images."

tive visualizations." Moreover, the deceased who has been prepared by the sacred funerary rites—of the Egyptians, for instance, or even of Achilles and Patroclus's homeland, Phthia—himself "is regarded as an animated statue and the statue is regarded as a mummy; both of them are transfigured forms and instruments of divine *heka** powers."[1] The often misunderstood opening of the mouth ceremony surviving from Fourth Dynasty Egypt, for example—a rite performed on both the deceased as well as a living initiate of the "House of Life"—is in fact just such a ritual of animation.[2] Furthermore, like the episode that Proclus used to illustrate the anagogic rite of theurgic elevation—for example, Achilles's funeral pyre for Patroclus—animated statues too can be found described within the Homeric epics.

Hephaestus, the son of Zeus and Hera and the god of craftsmen and volcanoes, is famous in Greek mythology for his abilities in *technikōs*—that is, specifically, his skill in making animated statues, called *automatons*. In the *Iliad,* the first of these mentioned are a set of twenty tripods, erected on golden wheels, that magically moved "of their own motion." A few lines later, Homer writes of a group of golden handmaidens Hephaestus also constructed that, in appearance, were "like living young women." "There is intelligence in their hearts, and there is speech in them and strength," the poet says of Hephaestus's maidens, "and from the immortal gods they have learned how to do things."[3]

> Made of gold, yet able to move rapidly [. . .] like young maidens, they are further endowed with [. . .] mind, voice, and strength, the three senses vital to early Greeks and taught to them by the gods.[4]

A third mention of animated statues appears in the *Odyssey* in regard to the palace of the "great-hearted Alkinoös," for which Hephaestus, in all "his craftsmanship and cunning," constructed golden and silver guard dogs to patrol the king's grounds. In all three of these cases, Homer has

---

**Heka* is the deity and force of magical power in ancient Egyptian cosmogony.

shown Hephaestus to be the prototypical animator of theurgic statues. "Surely," says Sarah P. Morris, a classicist and archaeologist, "these creatures are magic [. . .] in a way only possible in an Olympian setting, but marvels in a way only visible to mortal eyes."[5] However all of this may appear to the gentle reader, while Hephaestus's automatons may seem like it to the metamodern eye, animated statues are not to be confused with programmed, mechanical robots. To the ancient Greek mind, the *automata* were *animate*—that is, they were possessed of *anima,* of psyche or soul. That is not to say that such contrivances did not exist, only that said devices are not what we are here discussing. Aristotle's *thaumata,* or puppets, are a case in point.

In one of the more curious passages in his *Metaphysics A,* for example, Aristotle addresses the metaphysical problem of automata, self-moving thaumata. If these were merely mechanical, wind-up devices, their problem for the philosopher would not be metaphysical but would naturally be purely physical. Aristotle's choice of words here, too, is not accidental, for it is as thaumata that Plato, in his *Laws I,* considers man. Recalling the imagery of puppeteers from his "Allegory of the Cave," the Athenian says:

> [Let's] imagine that each of us living beings is a puppet of the gods. Whether we have been constructed to serve as their plaything, or for some serious reason, is something beyond our ken, but what we certainly do know is this: we have these emotions in us, which act like cords or strings and tug us about; they work in opposition, and tug against each other to make us perform actions that are opposed correspondingly; back and forth we go across the boundary line where vice and virtue meet.[6]

Like the Demiurge's creation in Plato's *Timaeus,* humans are described in the *Laws* as essentially agalmas—animated cult statues consecrated for use in a demiurgic rite that is acted out by the very gods themselves in what cultural historian Jeremy Naydler has called "the Temple of the Cosmos."[7] "[We] are images of intellective essences," says Proclus in his *Chaldæan Philosophy,* "but statues of the unknown *synthēmata.*"[8] Additionally, it must be noted that this "puppet-like body is turned into a living agalma only by the binding and animating power of 'soul' and 'intellect,'" Uždavinys reminds us "of [psyche] and [nous] respectively"[9]—and not by the mere *technikōs* of man. "The soul fashions itself as the cult statue,"[10] as Ilinca Tanaseanu-Döbler phrased it.

One of the most famous accounts of statue animation in antiquity comes to us from Eunapius and concerns the Neoplatonist Maximus of Ephesus and a statue of Hecate in her Pergamene shrine. "After convoking all his philosophical friends," Eunapius records that Maximus "offers a grain of incense, mutters a hymn and thus makes the cult statue smile and laugh; finally, the torches of the image flare up with fire."[11] Notably, Tanaseanu-Döbler sees in Eunapius's anecdote a potential allusion to the fiery, visionary references in fragments 146 through 148 of the *Chaldæan Oracles.*

Damascius, on the other hand, tells us that Heraiscus, an Egyptian Neoplatonist, had a natural gift of distinguishing between animate and inanimate cult statues.

He had but to look at one of them and immediately his heart was afflicted by divine frenzy while both his body and soul leapt up as if possessed by the god. But if he was not moved in such a way, the statue (*agalma*) was inanimate [. . .] and devoid of divine inspiration.[12]

"It was in this way that he recognized that the ineffable statue [. . .] of Aion was possessed by the god who was worshipped by the Alexandrians," Damascius adds, "being at the same time Osiris and Adonis as a result of a truly mystical act of union."[13] Far from priestly gimmicks and trickery, therefore, the business of animated cult statues was quite a serious one for our theurgic practitioners.

The key to telestikē in the form of theurgic statue animation is the successful contrivance of a proper *hypodochên* or fit receptacle that is capable of harnessing something of the divine ray with which the theurgist is attempting to work. Recall the quote from Plotinus (*Ennead* IV.3.11.1–7) given earlier in chapter 4:

> It seems to me that the sages of old who wanted to attract to themselves the presence of the gods, and built [. . .] statues to that end, looking to the nature of the universe, had in mind that the nature of the soul is a thing that is in general easy to attract, but the easiest way of all to receive it would be if one were to craft something sympathetic which was able to receive some share of it. And that is sympathetic which is in any way imitative of it, like a mirror able to catch some image of it.[14]

A receptacle is made "sympathetic" and "mirror-like" via the use of mysterious theurgic talismans called *synthēmata* (tokens) and *symbola* (symbols), which recapitulate and manifest the divine in miniature form upon the sensible plane—not unlike the way in which mathematical fractals reiterate the entire macrocosmic domain at microcosmic levels. To quote Edmonds, "[every] portion of the universe [. . .] has an element of divinity appropriate to it, [and] the divine stretches even to the lowest levels of created matter."[15] Accordingly, theurgic *synthēmata* and *symbola* do not simply stand for divine things, but in a sense are the "gods" themselves. "The *symbola* of the noetic realm are immanently woven into the very fabric of the material world," says Uždavinys, "and constitute its unifying divine foundation." They are, therefore, the means by which the transcendent *pēgē* or source maintains omnipresence or immanence in the sensible world. Fragment 108 of the *Chaldæan Oracles* says, for instance:

> For the Paternal Intellect has sown symbols [symbola] throughout the cosmos, (the Intellect) which thinks the intelligibles. And (these intelligibles) are called inexpressible beauties.[16]

Like Easter eggs hidden in a video game, *synthēmata* and *symbola* are "sown" throughout the cosmic landscape for the theurgist to engage and unlock their corresponding powers and abilities. Proclus explains:

The masters of hieratic art [. . .] have thus discovered how to gain the favour of powers above, mixing some things together and setting others apart in due order. They used mixing because they saw that each unmixed thing possesses some property of the god but is not enough to call that god forth. Therefore, by mixing many things they unified the aforementioned influences and made a unity generated from all of them similar to the whole that is prior to them all. And they often devised composite statues and fumigations, having blended separate signs together into one and having made artificially something embraced essentially by the divine through unification of many powers, the dividing of which makes each one feeble, while mixing raises it up to the form of the exemplar.[17]

The easiest way to think about synthēmata and symbola are as esoteric correspondences or theosophic signatures that "operate between all the levels of reality of the universe," which, as Antoine Faivre so eloquently explains it, "is a sort of theater of mirrors inhabited and animated by invisible forces."[18] Descending from each Platonic form a hierarchical seira (series) is envisaged, a chain of corresponding elements that reaches all the way through reality—from the most exalted to the most basic creatures and creations and throughout all the kingdoms of the created cosmos. Each link in a given seira corresponds to the archetypal form of that chain to the degree that the element in question participates (*methexis*) in its ruling Idea. Proclus provides us with an example of a solar seira, for instance, that encapsulates animals such as roosters and lions, plants including heliotropes and sunflowers, and minerals like the sunstone. Each of these elements partake "of some connection to the sun," Edmonds explains, "just as the visible sun itself is connected to the higher solar powers that transcend the perceptible world."[19] Proclus illustrates this as follows:

Why do heliotropes [. . .] move together with the Sun, selenotropes [. . .] with the Moon, moving around to the extent of their ability with the luminaries of the cosmos? All things pray according to their own order and sing hymns, either intellectually or rationally or naturally or sensibly, to heads of entire chains. And since the heliotrope is also moved toward that to which it readily opens, if anyone hears it striking the air as it moves about, he perceives in the sound that it offers to the King the kind of hymn that a plant can sing.[20]

Like a choir of Pythagorean sirens, the entire cosmos sings out the music of the spheres at each successive ontological plane. Iamblichus explains the receptacles, tokens, and symbols in this way:

> Observing this, and discovering in general, in accordance with the properties of each of the gods, the receptacles adapted to them, the theurgic art in many cases links together stones, plants, animals, aromatic substances, and other such things that are sacred, perfect and godlike, and then from all these composes an integrated and pure receptacle.[21]

An especially appropriate comparandum in this regard are the *minkisi* (*nkisi,* singular) of the Bantu-speaking people of West Central Africa and the *bilongo* or medicines that many of them contain. Among the slaves of Cuba, this Kongolese practice evolved into what is known as Palo Mayombe, a diasporic religion with multiple variants, including Palo Brillumba, Palo Kimbisa, and the more generic Palo Monte. Initiates in these religious practices are called *paleros* (male) and *paleras* (female). Nicholaj de Mattos Frisvold, a palero with a background in anthropology and in the science of religion, writes:

> The term nkisi [spirit pot/statue] was a particular form of medicine, a holy medicine that both encapsulated a part of the divine, but was a truly living, divinely-endowed talisman. [. . .] The nkisi was empowered by *bilongo,* the magical or active part of inspired nature, such as herbs, animals and minerals. The bilongo was placed at the heart of the figure and animated.[22]

Just as with symbols and tokens in telestikē, which particular bilongo the *nganga* (a Bantu ritual specialist) and palero uses in the construction of his nkisi is determined by the nature of the particular *mpungo* that rules the nkisi. The mpungos are akin to gods, powers, or archetypes.

> To this are added the *macutos* (charms/amulets), the *bilongos* (workings), the *mpolos* (powders), *firmas* [charaktēres], *mbele* (blade), the powders of the cat, the dog, the rooster, the vulture and the eagle. By conjuration and blood, the nkisi comes together as a lycanthropic creation that travels within earth as well as on the winds, the manifested powers of the primordial sorcerer [. . .] now named and conscious.[23]

One would be mistaken, however, to assume that synthēmata and symbola were merely intellectual correlations or a mnemonic system. Unlike Thelemic magician Charles Stansfeld Jones's kabbalistic Tree of Life, the cosmic agalma envisaged by the theurgist is not reducible to a simple "filing cabinet"[24] of correspondences. "*Sunthēmata* (signatures) inscribed in the soul through *logos* should simply not be confused at all with conventional signs that need to be sent, received and decoded in order to be interpreted and understood," Wouter Hanegraaff rightly insists. "It seems more adequate to think of them as activators of a presence that was believed to be always already there, but needed to be remembered or called back to conscious awareness: *nous,* the only ultimately true reality of Life and Light."[25] About this fact, to avoid any confusion, Iamblichus goes to great lengths to make himself perfectly clear:

> [It] is not pure thought that unites theurgists to the gods. Indeed what, then, would hinder those who are theoretical philosophers from enjoying a theurgic union with the gods? But the situation is not so: it is the accomplishments of acts not to be divulged and beyond all conception, and the power of the unutterable symbols,

understood solely by the gods, which establishes theurgic union. Hence, we do not bring about these things by intellection alone; for thus their efficiency would be intellectual, and dependent on us. But neither assumption is true. For even when we are not engaged in intellection, the symbols themselves, by themselves, perform their appropriate work, and the ineffable power of the gods, to whom these symbols relate, itself recognizes the proper images of itself, not through being aroused by our thought.[26]

Like psychoactive drugs, the resultant effect(s) of theurgic engagement with synthēmata and symbola have the potential to manifest in one's consciousness—that is, they have the potential to awaken their corresponding *logoi* within the soul—whether or not he knows to anticipate those effects. It doesn't take rational discourse to render synthēmata and symbola potent or effective. Truly, they are effective by their very existence. If fact, one might even say that true theurgy and telestikē begin at the precise juncture where logic and discursive reasoning end. As Chlup correctly observes:

> If the theurgists attribute great power to soulless objects, which are the lowest and simplest terms in our world, it is precisely because these are easiest to use for evoking the divine potency that by its simplicity surpasses all rational insights.[27]

Perhaps the most accessible example of statue animation in the ancient world comes from the *Chaldæan Oracles*. In fragment 224, the goddess Hecate instructs her worshippers in practical telestikē.

> But execute my statue, purifying it as I shall instruct you. Make a form from wild rue and decorate it with small animals, such as lizards which live about the house. Rub a mixture of myrrh, gum, and frankincense with these animals, and out in the clear air under the waxing moon, complete [telei] this (statue) yourself while offering the following prayer.[28]

Let us take a moment to scrutinize the constituents of this magical recipe. As the reader may have gathered, all of the ingredients for which this statue spell calls—wild rue, lizards, certain tree resins, the waxing moon, and so on—are tokens (synthēmata) and symbols (symbola) associated with the goddess Hecate. The majority of them, it will be noted, are psychoactive.

The first ingredient listed in the *Chaldæan Oracles'* recipe is wild rue. According to Pliny the Elder,

> [t]he cultivated kind [of rue] has broader leaves and more numerous branches than the other. Wild rue is more violent in its effects, and more active in every respect. The juice of it is extracted by beating it up, and moistening it moderately with water; after which it is kept for use in boxes of Cyprian copper. Given in large doses, this juice has all the baneful effects of poison [. . .] The most efficacious, however, of all, is the root of wild rue, taken with wine; this too, it is said, is more beneficial still, if drunk in the open air.[29]

As the Roman historian illustrates, the ancients distinguished between two types of rue, cultivated and wild. Cultivated rue refers to *Ruta graveolens,* a common plant that was known to and valued by the Romans as an additive to wine on account of its rich bouquet. Based on Pliny's description of wild rue, it is clear that an intoxicating substance may be indicated. Moreover, Pliny tellingly associates rue with vision.

> [Engravers] and painters are in the habit of eating it with bread, or else nasturtium, for the benefit of the sight; wild goats, too, eat it for the sight, they say. Many persons have dispersed films on the eyes by rubbing them with a mixture of the juice of rue with Attic honey, or the milk of a woman just delivered of a male child: the same result has been produced also by touching the corners of the eyes with the pure juice of the plant.[30]

In his 1554 work, *Des Cruydboeks,* Flemish physician and botanist Rembert Dodoens identified Pliny's wild rue as none other than Syrian rue (*Peganum harmala*), an entheogenic plant with known monoamine oxidase inhibitor (MAOI) content—not unlike the legendary ayahuasca vine, *Banisteriopsis caapi*—and a long history of ritual use.[31] In the Middle East, for instance, the seeds of Syrian rue are incinerated to this day as an apotropaic device against the evil eye.[32]

The next ingredient for which Hecate's Chaldæan recipe calls is lizards. Fascinatingly, in 1996, a farmhouse excavated near Pompeii in Naples, Italy, from around 79 CE, revealed a number of intact *dolia* or storage vats used for fermenting wine. Inside one of the vats was discovered a residue containing remnants of a number of plants, some of them entheogenic, including *Papaver somniferum,* the infamous opium poppy. Significantly, alongside the dolia was discovered an assemblage of bones, belonging to frogs, toads, and, yes, even lizards. The author of the study, archaeologist Marina Ciaraldi, compared the Pompeii concoction to a well-known potion called *mithridatium,* containing both opium and lizards, which took its name from Mithridates IV, king of Pontus (120–63 BCE). While Pliny lists at least forty-four ingredients that can be combined to produce the potion, a notebook discovered in Mithridates's palace names only four, including "leaves of rue."[33] Provided what we know about the rue referenced in the *Chaldæan Oracles* in connection with Hecate, it is likely that this is also a case of "wild rue." Lizards, on the other hand, are a known common ingredient in ancient philters or love potions, to which intoxicating plants, such as opium and mandrake, were often added. The second-century Roman novelist Apuleius, for example, spoke of them when he wrote:

> *They dig out all kinds of philtres*
> *from everywhere:*
> *they search for the agent that*
> *arouses mutual love:*
> *pills and nails and threads,*

roots and herbs and shoots,
the two-tailed lizard,
and charms from mares.[34]

In the practice of the aforementioned Africa-inspired practice of Palo Mayombe, there is no question in regard to the occult nature of the "lizard." Todd Ramón Ochoa, an associate professor in the Department of Religious Studies at the University of North Carolina, Chapel Hill, relates that:

> when pests [. . .] begin to overtake the house of an old person, they do so as heralds of the old one's death. Lizards soon follow to prey on the insects. When these come it is understood that death is inevitable. That a progressing infestation accompanies the weakening of an old person would seem obvious and that bugs and lizards are thus considered privileged associates of death, its heralds and its avatars, makes practical sense.[35]

Thus, "lizards which live about the house" may be viewed as ambassadors of the liminal plane betwixt the living and the dead—the daimonic domain of the goddess Hecate. Notably, lizards are called for in no less than eleven of the spells preserved in the *PGM*.

While there are no extant lizards or salamanders that are possessed of known entheogenic compounds, there are a number of species in the animal kingdom with pronounced inebriating qualities. The Colorado River toad (*Incilius alvarius,* formerly *Bufo alvarius*), for example, famously secretes 5-MeO-Dimethyltryptamine (5-MeO-DMT) from its parotid glands. Given that this species is in danger of extinction because of too many people eagerly "milking" the toads to acquire their potent psychoactive excretions, it is not inconceivable that a similarly entheogenic species of reptile or amphibian may have existed in Europe at one time in the past but has since gone extinct for a similar reason.

Significantly, a 2014 paper published by Roshan Bhad et al. titled "The Lizard: An Unconventional Psychoactive Substance?" reports on a thirty-year-old opiate-dependent Indian male with a two- to three-lizard-a-day habit. The Indian wall lizard or common house gecko (*Hemidactylus flaviviridis*) is regularly found in many Indian households. According to the authors of the paper, the opiate-dependent man:

> reported that he started using tail of wall lizard from past 10 years after one seer introduced it in the smoking form, filled in an earthen pipe (chillum) along with ganja. He enjoyed the pleasurable effect and started using it to get high. The most frequent pattern of use was mixing burned tail of wall lizard in cigarette half filled with tobacco and smoking it. Occasionally, he claims to have consumed orally too, either by burning the tail of wall lizard to char or eating it raw after killing. He would usually consume 2–3 tails of wall lizards/week and maximum up to 2–3 tails of wall lizards/d. Patient claims the effect [. . .] would last longer and he would experience more euphoria after taking tail of wall lizard. [. . .] The subjective effects reported by him were increase self-esteem, confidence, and mild sedation that would last for 10–12 h. [. . .] He would usually obtain lizards from walls of the houses.[36]

Similarly, the Indian spiny-tailed lizard (*Uromastyx hardwickii*) is regularly hunted by locals to this day in the belief that the oil extracted from the fat is a natural aphrodisiac.[37] And in Africa, the powdered remains of the phallic-shaped *Lacerta scincus* lizard are imbibed as a local aphrodisiac.

In addition to using lizards as a love potion ingredient, the ancient Greeks also employed them to treat afflictions of the eyes.

> Lizards, also, are employed in numerous ways as a remedy for diseases of the eyes. Some persons enclose a green lizard in a new earthen vessel, together with nine of the small stones. [. . .] Upon each of these stones they make nine marks, and remove one from the vessel daily, taking care, when the ninth day is come, to let the lizard go, the stones being kept as a remedy for affections of the eyes.

Others, again, blind a green lizard, and after putting some earth beneath it, enclose it in a glass vessel, with some small rings of solid iron or gold. When they find, by looking through the glass, that the lizard has recovered its sight, they set it at liberty, and keep the rings as a preservative against ophthalmia. Others employ the ashes of a lizard's head as a substitute for antimony, for the treatment of eruptions of the eyes. Some recommend the ashes of the green lizard with a long neck that is usually found in sandy soils, as an application for incipient defluxions of the eyes, and for glaucoma. They say, too, that if the eyes of a [lizard] are extracted with a pointed instrument, its sight will return. [. . .] For continuous watering of the eyes, the ashes of a spotted lizard's head, applied with antimony, are remarkably efficacious.[38]

Confusingly, the word *lizards* may not refer to reptiles at all. According to Mariel Tishma, assistant editor of *Hekteon International: A Journal of Medical Humanities,* the use of lizard parts in ancient concoctions may allude instead to "ivy and other creeping plants."[39]

Herbalists may have used these folk names in an attempt to protect their practice. One ancient "spell book" explains that misleading names were chosen for ingredients due to "the curiosity of the masses." The general public, the writers believed, "do not take precaution" when using herbal cures or magic, and so must be discouraged by using frightening or disgusting names.[40]

Kristen Dzwiza, an archaeologist with a research focus in ancient Egyptian, Greek, and Roman magic, comments on this tendency:

In ancient spell instructions, individual ritual ingredients were coded in order to make the effectiveness of a ritual accessible only to the initiated. One possibility was the use of secret alphabets. Another—less known—was the use of code names. Examples of this are preserved in a magic papyrus from the 4th century

(PGM XII, 409 pp.), in which the author breaks down some of these codings:

"Blood of a snake" means bloodstone,

"Bone of an Ibis" is buckthorn,

"Semen of Hermes" is dill,

"Semen of Heracles" is mustard-rocket,

"Blood of a goose" is a mulberry tree's "milk,"

"A hawk's heart" is heart of wormwood.

It is noticeable that plants and valuable stones were coded with animal components.[41]

The ivy as intoxicant has been associated with Dionysus, the "god of madness," and his followers. The pinecone-capped fennel *thyrsis,* a staff ceremonially carried by the frenzied followers of Dionysus, was entwined with ivy. It is said that Dionysus, before his discovery of wine, ate toxic ivy berries for the purpose of intoxication. In Plutarch's *Quaestiones Romanae,* the Middle Platonist and priest of Delphi mentions the manic *maenads,* the female followers of Dionysus, and their strange use of "ivy" to achieve *enthousiasmos*—the ancient Greek word from which Ruck et al. famously derived the term *entheogen.*

But to complicate matters, it is not always clear what species of ivy is being indicated or even if the plant referenced is indeed ivy and not some other botanical. Psychedelic historians Eden Woodruff and Thomas Hatsis explain:

Plutarch's description clearly points towards an entheogenic plant when he writes that the ivy causes a "wineless drunkenness and joyousness" in those who consume it; and yet, we know of no kind of ivy today that would cause such effects.

Could it be that the ancient Greeks over-harvested the ivy to the point of extinction? Or perhaps "ivy" could have been a local name for a plant like opium or mandrake (much the same way some people refer to cannabis as "weed" today). It's enough to make one wonder what other substances have been lost to us through the uncompromising ruins of time for one reason or another.[42]

Australian psychedelic researcher Snu Voogelbreinder in his impressive study *Garden of Eden: The Shamanic Use of Psychoactive Flora and Fauna, and the Study of Consciousness* reports that although common ivy (*Hedera helix*) has certainly been shown to have narcotic effects in both mice and rats and "has long been rumored to be psychoactive" in humans, the implied species in these ancient accounts may in fact be a variety of *Argyreia* or *Ipomoea,* such as Hawaiian baby woodrose or heavenly blue morning glories, each of which resemble ivy when not in flower. These plants are rich in the psychoactive alkaloid LSA (d-lysergic acid amide), also called ergine.[43] Voogelbreinder also notes that one common name for the potentiating passionflower (*Passiflora incarnata*) vine—which, like Syrian rue, is possessed of an MAOI—is ground ivy.[44] On the other hand, it's quite possible that "ivy" simply meant just that.

The next three ingredients, "myrrh, [Arabic] gum, and frankincense," each consist of saps collected from various trees, including *Comminphora myrrha, Acacia nilotica* and *senegal,* and *Boswellia sacra* and *carterii,* respectively. While Arabic gum is not psychoactive, both *Acacia nilotica* and *senegal* (the trees from which Arabic gum is collected) are possessed of the powerful serotonergic entheogen, N,N-Dimethyltryptamine (N,N-DMT). The other two ingredients, on the other hand, deserve some treatment. As Danny Nemu, a psychedelic researcher with an academic background in the history and philosophy of medicine, points out in his paper "Getting High with the Most High: Entheogens in the Old Testament":

> *C. myrrha* (myrrh) contains among its components large amounts of the furanosesquiterpenoids 2-acetoxyfuranodiene (9.80%), furanoeudesma-1,3-diene (8.97%), curzerene (6.71%–17%) and furanodiene, as well as α-pinene, limonene, cuminaldehyde, eugenol, safrole, myrcene, and elemicin.[45]

The bioactive compounds in myrrh, called furano-sesquiterpenoids, are active at μ-opioid and δ-opioid receptors, with a noted potency of 10 percent to that of morphine. Moreover, according to Al-Hasani and Bruchas's 2011 study, "molecular mechanisms of opioid receptor-dependent signaling and behavior" curzarene, furanodiene, and furanoeudesma-1,3-diene have all three also been found to be effective mood enhancers, causing activation of the central dopamine reward pathways that modulate euphoria.[46] Similarly, limonene, a terpene that myrrh shares with cannabis, has been shown to increase both serotonin and dopamine levels in areas of the brain associated with anxiety, depression, and even obsessive-compulsive disorder (OCD).[47] Eugenol, a terpene found in cloves, and elemicin, a compound found in nutmeg, are each classified as sedatives, while safrole, also found in nutmeg, is a precursor to 3,4-Methylenedioxymethamphetamine (MDMA) and was classified by Bourgeois et al. as a hallucinogen.[48] In regard to frankincense, Nemu continues:

> The dehydroabietic acid component [of frankincense] is a GABA-receptor modulator with tranquillizing, anti-depressant, and anxiolytic actions in mice. [. . .] Other components [. . .] include α- and β-pinene, camphene, sabinene, myrcene, limonene, and linalool.[49]

As stated above, limonene increases both serotonin and dopamine levels, while β-pinene, another terpene shared with some strains of cannabis, was, like safrole, classified by Bourgeois et al. as a hallucinogen.

Ergo, virtually every synthēmata and symbola called for in the animation of Hecate's statue in the *Chaldæan Oracles* constitutes *phármaka* and has the potential to drastically alter one's state of consciousness. Obviously, from Polydamna's *nēpenthés phármakon*[50] or "anti-sorrow drug-charm," to the episode on the isle of the gentle Lotus-eaters,[51] to the magical therianthropic potion of the witch Circe[52]—whose Homeric epithet happens to be *polyphármakos,* "skilled in many drugs or charms,"[53] we might add—*phármaka* was not unknown to the author(s) of the Homeric epics either.

Regarding the prayer that is to be offered for the completion (*telei*) of the Hecate statue, the *Oracles* are silent. However, in his tome *Refutation of All Heresies*, Hippolytus of Rome preserves the following prayer from Proclus, who penned an entire commentary on the *Chaldæan Oracles*, which just so happens to concern the animation of a Hecate statue.

> *Approach, you of the netherworld, of earth, and of*
> *   heaven, Growler!*
> *You by the wayside, at the crossroads, light-bearer,*
> *   night-wanderer,*
> *Enemy of light, friend and companion of night,*
> *Rejoicing in the bark of pups and in bright red blood,*
> *Lurking among the corpses and the tombs of the dead,*
> *Lusting for blood, bringing terror to mortals,*
> *Grim one, Ogress, Moon—you of many forms,*
> *May you come gracious to our immolations!*[54]

"When he says this," Hippolytus adds, "fire is seen tearing through the air."

In the way that only he can, Uždavinys sums up telestikē in the following manner:

> In the context of Hellenic cultic practice, [. . .] the statue (*agalma*) is regarded as a vessel and container for the divine powers that take up residence inside it. The awakening of these powers is sometimes achieved by the practice of putting *pharmaka* (remedies, drugs, herbs, magical means of power, charms, enchantments, symbols) into hollow statues and thereby animating them.[55]

> Both the cult statue and the human body may be regarded as privileged habitations for the god (or the immortal *nous*). Therefore, just as the priest fills the interior of an *agalma* with *sumbola*, *sunthemata*, and *pharmaka*, while uttering verbal formulas and thereby animating the statue (making it *empnoös*), so the spiritual path of inner transformation, followed by the initiate,

results in the awakening of those *sunthemata* which the Demiurge concealed within his soul and body.[56]

[Compare] the animated statues which contain both visible and invisible *sunthemata* (also regarded as *pharmaka*—drugs, charms, secret means) of the gods to the entire sensible universe which is constructed like a statue by the Demiurge and contains all kinds of visible and invisible *sumbola* of the noetic and supra-noetic realms.[57]

CONCLUSION

We have arrived at the end of our analysis of the theory and praxis of theurgy as viewed through a Homeric lens by the Neoplatonists. We have seen that, not unlike the soul flights of some of the earliest Greek philosophers, theurgic practitioners continued the variety of discorporation associated primarily with the shamans of central and northeast Asia. Among the so-called Presocratics, this soul flight manifested in the form of katabatic trips to the underworld. However, by the time we arrive at Plato and his Athenian master, Socrates, while the motif of soul flight remained, the orientation of that flight shifted in favor of anabasis—a preoccupation that would persist right through the era of the Middle Platonists and the *Chaldæan Oracles* to the time of the theurgic Neoplatonists of late antiquity.

Significantly, however, Neoplatonists such as Porphyry of Tyre and Proclus Lycius were wont to project the origins of theurgy onto the Homeric epics, rather than identifying the paradigm of theurgy within the *Chaldæan Oracles* or even in Plato. As we have labored to demonstrate in this book, such a projection is not unwarranted. In the case of Porphyry, the philosophical theory underlying theurgy was envisaged as being encoded in Book XIII of the *Odyssey*, with Homer's description of Odysseus's discovery of the Cave of the Nymphs in the port of Phorcys. There, following Numenius's lead, Porphyry believed he identified an ancient, encrypted literary illustration showing the esoteric blueprint—replete with points of entry and exit—of the sensible, created cosmos. In Proclus's case, the technical praxis of theurgy was understood as having its beginnings within the Phthian funeral rite performed by Achilles for Patroclus, as recorded in Book XXIII of the *Iliad*. For Proclus, as for his master (Syrianus), Achilles was regarded as "the prototype of the theurgical officiant"—that is, as the "priest or master of the initiation," while Patroclus "resembles the initiate who has undergone a symbolic death and burial"—in other words, he resembles the "aspirant who is to be initiated into the mysteries and his soul separated by certain 'sacred methods.'"[1]

Finally, we saw that even the curious art of agalma or statue animation in the West—a form of telestikē practiced by both the theurgists and Hermetists alike—too can be traced all the way back to the blind bard. The Neoplatonists were therefore not simply inventing or imagining nonexistent connections between the epics and themselves, but rather were possessed of ample reason to maintain that the art of theurgy did in fact originate, or at least continue, with Homer and his immortal epics.

APPENDIX
HOMEROMANTEION

A *Method of Bibliomancy from the* Greek Magical Papyri *Involving the* Iliad, *the* Odyssey, *and* Astragaloi *or* Kuboi

Where man regularly articulated his *aspirations* to the gods in the form of prayer, in ancient Greece, it was often through the use of powerful oracular devices that he received divine *inspirations* directly from them. One variety of oracular device was a collection of techniques and corresponding texts known as *Homeromanteia* or "Oracles of Homer"— divinatory practices involving the reliance on Homeric texts for oracular pronouncements. The particular *Homeromanteion** we've included here was preserved in the *Greek Magical Papyri* or *Papyri Graecae Magicae* (*PGM* VII.1–148)[1] and involves the use of one or three *astragaloi* (sheep knuckles) or *kuboi* (dice), both of which are possessed of six sides with as many numbers. The astragaloi or kuboi are thrown to select a set of three random numbers (if only one knuckle or dice is employed, it must

---

*All translations have been traded out in favor of those of Lattimore.

be thrown thrice) which are then matched to a correlating line, apparently randomly arranged, from Homer's *Iliad* and *Odyssey*—generally selected from proverbial narrations pronounced by either gods or heroes. One third- or fourth-century Homeromanteion from Oxyrhynchus explains the method.

> First, you must known the days on which to use the Oracle, you must pray and speak the incantation of the god and pray inwardly for what you want; third, you must take the die and throw it three times and having thrown consult the Oracle according to the number of the three [throws] of the die, as it is composed.[2]

1-1-1   life, but still for the sake of the cursed stomach people [*Od.* XV.344]

1-1-2   nor anchor stones to be thrown ashore nor cables to make fast; [*Od.* IX.137]

1-1-3   rose as they were struck with the sword, and the water was reddened [*Il.* XXI.21]

1-1-4   ...

1-1-5   stood up holding the scepter Hephaistos had wrought him carefully. [*Il.* II.101]

1-1-6   ...

1-2-1   I am willing to make all good, and give back gifts in abundance. : I am willing to make all good and give back gifts in abundance. [*Il.* IX.120; XIX.138]

1-2-2   it is the very gods who ruined the brain within you. : it is the very gods who ruined the brain within you, [*Il.* VII.360; XII.234]

1-2-3   ...

1-2-4   ...

1-2-5   in your dear mother's keeping; and I hope you come back rejoicing [*Od.* XV.128]

1-2-6   ...

1-3-1   ...

1-3-2   ...

1-3-3   But Zeus does not bring to accomplishment all thoughts in men's minds. [*Il.* XVIII.328]

1-3-4   Truly I could have wished it so; it would be far better : presents, that would be what I wished, there would be much advantage : then that would be my wish also, since it would be far better [*Il.* III.41; *Od.* XI.358; XX.316]

1-3-5   so, Melanthios, he would send flying all those glories [*Od.* XVII.244]

1-3-6   things are in my mind also, lady; yet I would feel deep shame [*Il.* VI.441]

1-4-1   ...

1-4-2   him fair, but in the deep of their hearts were devising evils. [*Od.* XVII.66]

1-4-3   Never to be cast away are the gifts of the gods, magnificent, [*Il.* III.65]

1-4-4   ...

1-4-5   ...

1-4-6   "All this, illustrious Skamandros, shall be as you order. [*Il.* XXI.223]

1-5-1   to yourself a thing shameful but bringing joy to the enemy? [*Il.* III.51]

1-5-2   Sometime within this very year Odysseus will be here. : Sometime within this very year Odysseus will be here, [*Od.* XIV.161; XIX.306]

1-5-3   no use to you, since you will never be laid away in them; [*Il.* XXII.513]

1-5-4   Let the woman go to the winner, and all the possessions.
         [*Il.* III.255]

1-5-5   Lordship for many is no good thing. Let there be one ruler,
         [*Il.* II.204]

1-5-6   All the forecourt is huddled with ghosts, the yard is full of
         them [*Od.* XX.355]

1-6-1   We have won ourselves enormous fame; we have killed the great
         Hektor [*Il.* XXII.393]

1-6-2   "Who would take upon him this work and bring it to
         fulfillment [*Il.* X.303]

1-6-3   not if he gave me gifts as many as the sand or the dust is,
         [*Il.* IX.385]

1-6-4   ...

1-6-5   ...

1-6-6   ...

2-1-1   for there is no one of the islands that has meadows for driving
         horses; [*Od.* IV.607]

2-1-2   to what you heard from your fathers before you, when you were
         children, [*Od.* IV.688]

2-1-3   ...

2-1-4   ...

2-1-5   ...

2-1-6   I hate his gifts. I hold him light as the strip of a splinter.
         [*Il.* IX.378]

2-2-1   who is a single child brought among many possessions. : when
         he comes back in the tenth year from a distant country,
         [*Il.* IX.482; *Od.* XVI.19 (?)]

2-2-2   ...

2-2-3   ...

2-2-4   ...

2-2-5 So these were gathered around Achilleus, and now came to them [*Od.* XXIV.19]

2-2-6 lying stories, from which no one could learn anything. You have [*Od.* XI.366]

2-3-1 be bold also, so that in generations to come they will praise you. [*Od.* I.302]

2-3-2 leaning against the column, work of men's hand, on the gravemound [*Il.* XI.371]

2-3-3 go. The way is there, and next to the water are standing [*Il.* IX.43]

2-3-4 'You will be a liar, not put fulfillment on what you have spoken. [*Il.* XIX.107]

2-3-5 And side by side with him his mother in tears was mourning [*Il.* XXII.79]

2-3-6 not if you were to sit beside me five years, and six years, [*Od.* III.115]

2-4-1 So he spoke, and told Paiëon to heal him; and scattering [*Il.* V.899]

2-4-2 "All this, my unhappy friend, I will do for you as you ask me." [*Od.* XI.80]

2-4-3 How can you wish to make wasted and fruitless all this endeavor, [*Il.* IV.26]

2-4-4 late to be accomplished, whose glory shall perish never. [*Il.* II.325]

2-4-5 sooner you would be tired of it and go back to your country. [*Od.* III.117]

2-4-6 corn land, so that thence he can bring back poisonous medicines [*Od.* II.329]

2-5-1 "My husband, you were lost young from life, and have left me [*Il.* XXIV.725]

2-5-2 the way I think, and the way it will be accomplished, that you may not [*Il.* IX.310 (?)]

2-5-3   "My honored mother, lift not to me the kindly sweet wine, [*Il*. VI.264]

2-5-4   ...

2-5-5   ...

2-5-6   glittered as they marched the shining armor they carried. [*Il*. VI.432]

2-6-1   here, whether coming to court me or meeting for some other reason? [*Od*. IV.685]

2-6-2   He should not sleep night long who is a man burdened with counsels [*Il*. II.24]

2-6-3   "Strange man! It is not fair to keep in your heart this coldness. [*Il*. VI.326]

2-6-4   Who knows whether he will come someday and punish the violence [*Od*. III.216]

2-6-5   then I shall get wives for you both, and grant you possessions [*Od*. XXI.214]

2-6-6   with fat, can then attempt to bend it, and finish the contest. [*Od*. XXI.180]

3-1-1   There is no shame in running, even by night, from disaster. [*Il*. XIV.80]

3-1-2   Remember every valor of yours, for now the need comes [*Il*. XXII.268]

3-1-3   a widow in your house, and the boy is only a baby : a widow in your house, and the boy is only a baby [*Il*. XXII.484; cf. XXIV.726]

3-1-4   Therefore do not yet go into the grind of the war god, [*Il*. XVIII.134]

3-1-5   for in misfortune mortal men grow old more suddenly.' [*Od*. XIX.360]

3-1-6   ...

3-2-1   ...

3-2-2   There is no such man living nor can there ever be one [*Od.* VI.201]

3-2-3   "Yes, it is true, my child, this is no cowardly action,
         [*Il.* XVIII.128]

3-2-4   Now there is no way for him to get clear away from us,
         [*Il.* XXII.219]

3-2-5   set them free for bronze and gold; it is there inside, since
         [*Il.* XXII.50]

3-2-6   and drink your wine, nor quarrel with men who are younger
         than you [*Od.* XXI.310]

3-3-1   where are you running, turning your back in battle like a
         coward? [*Il.* VIII.94]

3-3-2   If only the man to be called my husband could be like this one,
         [*Od.* VI.244]

3-3-3   grows until she strides on the earth with her head striking
         heaven. [*Il.* IV.443]

3-3-4   But Zeus does not bring to accomplishment all thoughts in
         men's minds. [*Il.* XVIII.328]

3-3-5   and bent his head, that the people should stay alive, and not
         perish. [*Il.* VIII.246]

3-3-6   I wish you had not supplicated the blameless son of Peleus
         [*Il.* IX.698]

3-4-1   talk. The honeyed wine has hurt you, as it has distracted
         [*Od.* XXI.293]

3-4-2   Act as your purpose would have you do, and hold back no
         longer." [*Il.* XXII.185]

3-4-3   Thus it is destiny for us both to stain the same soil [*Il.* XVIII.329]

3-4-4   strike so; thus you may be a light given to the Danaäns,
         [*Il.* VIII.282]

3-4-5   you have done to me. So there is no one who can hold the dogs
         off [*Il.* XXII.348]

3-4-6   You will never kill me. I am not one who is fated."
         [*Il.* XXII.13]

3-5-1 you would stay here with me and be the lord of this household [*Od.* V.208]

3-5-2 'Give way, old sir, from the forecourt, before you are taken and dragged [*Od.* XVIII.10]

3-5-3 The man does better who runs from disaster than he who is caught by it." [*Il.* XIV.81]

3-5-4 all, and tell no one out of all the men and the women [*Od.* XIII.308]

3-5-5 for a man blessed in substance, and the cut swathes drop showering, [*Il.* XI.69]

3-5-6 The sort of thing you say is the thing that will be said to you. [*Il.* XX.250]

3-6-1 he had opposed the return of Helen to fair-haired Menelaos. [*Il.* XI.125]

3-6-2 Or will you change a little? The hearts of the great can be changed. [*Il.* XV.203]

3-6-3 And I never did have any doubt, but in my heart always [*Od.* XIII.339]

3-6-4 'It will not happen that way, Eurymachos. You yourself know this. [*Od.* XXI.257]

3-6-5 Ktesippos was his name, and he had his home in Same. [*Od.* XXI.288]

3-6-6 The father granted him one prayer, and denied him the other. [*Il.* XVI.250]

4-1-1 Go therefore back to the house, and take up your work, [*Od.* I.356]

4-1-2 these things for your wife, so you may tell her hereafter." [*Od.* XI.224 (alternate version)]

4-1-3 you had worn a mantle of flying stones for the wrong you did us." [*Il.* III.57]

4-1-4 prayed the immortals, beyond all else, to see him bearded.' [*Od.* XVIII.176]

4-1-5   but make your prayer to Apollo the light-born, the glorious archer, [*Il.* IV.101]

4-1-6   nor wolves and lambs have spirit that can be brought to agreement [*Il.* XXII.263]

4-2-1   Come then, in this thing let us both give way to each other, [*Il.* IV.62]

4-2-2   and Hate was there with Confusion among them, and Death the destructive; [*Il.* XVIII.535]

4-2-3   ...

4-2-4   Rise up then to battle, be such as you claimed in time past." [*Il.* IV.264]

4-2-5   ...

4-2-6   Fool, then why do you wear that bow, which is wind and nothing. [*Il.* XXI.474]

4-3-1   For even Niobē, she of lovely tresses, remembered [*Il.* XXIV.602]

4-3-2   bestowing bronze and gold in abundance upon him, and clothing, [*Od.* V.38]

4-3-3   Your journey then will be no vain thing nor go unaccomplished. [*Od.* II.273]

4-3-4   One bird sign is best: to fight in defense of our country. [*Il.* XII.243]

4-3-5   the yoke. I will drench her horns in gold and offer her to you." [*Il.* X.294]

4-3-6   and win you glory and gratitude in the sight of all Trojans, [*Il.* IV.95]

4-4-1   secretly, not in the open. There is no trusting in women. [*Od.* XI.456]

4-4-2   "I cannot, and I must not deny this thing that you ask for, [*Il.* XIV.212]

4-4-3   must at once turn his mind so it follows your heart, and my heart. [*Il.* XV.52]

4-4-4   This is what the old man told you, you have forgotten. Yet even
        [*Il.* XI.789]

4-4-5   glory, and hive your soul to Hades of the famed horses."
        [*Il.* V.654]

4-4-6   let him go to his ship and load it deep as he pleases [*Il.* IX.137]

4-5-1   Tell her part of it, but let the rest be hidden in silence.
        [*Od.* XI.443]

4-5-2   that Zeus cast on us as we were born this burden of evil." [*Il.* X.71]

4-5-3   even after death, but the rest of them are flittering shadows."
        [*Od.* X.495]

4-5-4   from the Aitolians; yet these no longer would make good
        [*Il.* IX.598]

4-5-5   "Hearing what you gave said, son of Laërtes, I am pleased with
        you. [*Il.* XIX.185]

4-5-6   Zeus builds up and Zeus diminishes the strength in men,
        [*Il.* XX.242]

4-6-1   Then in turn the Gerenian horseman Nestor answered him:
        [*Il.* XI.654]

4-6-2   in all haste; since now you might take the wide-wayed city
        [*Il.* II.66]

4-6-3   'Bear up, my heart. You have had worse to endure before this
        [*Od.* XX.18]

4-6-4   "Excellency! Sit still and listen to what others tell you, [*Il.* II.200]

4-6-5   had thrown away his anger and chosen the way of friendship.
        [*Il.* XVI.282]

4-6-6   so it is good, when a man has perished, to have a son left
        [*Od.* III.196]

5-1-1   And here, take this veil, it is immortal, and fasten it under
        [*Od.* V.346]

5-1-2   the cry. It is not piety to glory so over slain men. [*Od.* XXII.412]

5-1-3 through the immortal night while other mortals are sleeping? [*Il.* XXIV.363]

5-1-4 How could I forget Odysseus the godlike, he who [*Od.* I.65]

5-1-5 and destiny the powerful took hold of both eyes. [*Il.* V.83]

5-1-6 So there is nothing more deadly or more vile than a woman [*Od.* XI.427]

5-2-1 Let us not go on and fight the Danaäns by their ships. I think [*Il.* XII.216]

5-2-2 For I am Achilleus' henchman, and the same strong-wrought vessel : to defend a man, if anyone else picks a quarrel with him; : to defend myself against a man who has started a quarrel. [*Il.* XXIV.396; *Od.* XVI.72; XXI.133]

5-2-3 his children do not gather to his knees to welcome their father [*Il.* V.408]

5-2-4 'I am he. I am here in my house. After many sufferings [*Od.* XXI.207]

5-2-5 "Speak no more this way; there will be no time for changing [*Il.* V.218]

5-2-6 stay here the while, though he lean very hard toward the work of the war god, [*Il.* XIX.189]

5-3-1 You must not, in the pride of fury and fighting, go on [*Il.* XVI.91]

5-3-2 that I never entered into her bed and never lay with her : that he never entered into her bed and never lay with her [*Il.* IX.133; XIX.176]

5-3-3 enough to moisten the lips, not enough to moisten his palate. [*Il.* XXII.495]

5-3-4 "Do not fear. Let not these things be a thought in your mind. [*Il.* XVIII.463]

5-3-5 fighters; yet still I am not able to hit this mad dog." [*Il.* VIII.299]

5-3-6 "Friend, stay quiet rather and do as I tell you; I will [*Il.* IV.412]

5-4-1 'No virtue in bad dealings. See, the slow one has overtaken [*Od.* VIII.329]

5-4-2   to bar the tightly fitted doors that close the hall; tell them, [*Od.* XXI.236]

5-4-3   There is no thought of death in your mind now, and yet death stands [*Il.* XVII.201]

5-4-4   Odysseus is here, he is in the house, though late in his coming; [*Od.* XXIII.7]

5-4-5   late will he bring it to pass, and they must pay a great penalty, [*Il.* IV.161]

5-4-6   and Hatred is there, and Battle Strength, and heart-freezing Onslaught [*Il.* V.740]

5-5-1   but hunger is the sorriest way to die and encounter [*Od.* XII.342]

5-5-2   shall lie still, when I am dead. Now I must win excellent glory, [*Il.* XVIII.121]

5-5-3   Rise up then to battle, be such as you claimed in times past." [*Il.* IV.264]

5-5-4   'I am not insulting you, dear child. It is all true. [*Od.* XXIII.26]

5-5-5   and stayed the childbirth of Alkmeme, and held back the birth pangs. [*Il.* XIX.119]

5-5-6   Come now, I will make it good hereafter, if anything evil [*Il.* IV.362]

5-6-1   'Where so furious? How can your hearts so storm within you? [*Il.* VIII.413]

5-6-2   'Let him not be too much on your mind. It was I myself [*Od.* XIII.421]

5-6-3   But the gods give to mortals not everything at the same time; [*Il.* IV.320]

5-6-4   "Speak no more this way; there will be no time for changing [*Il.* V.218]

5-6-5   He spoke, but by such talk did not persuade the heart of Zeus [*Il.* XII.173]

5-6-6   but Odysseus stopped him, though he was eager, making a signal [*Od.* XXI.129]

6-1-1   How can you wish to go alone to the ships of the Achaians
[*Il.* XXIV.203]

6-1-2   married but without sons in his hall, leaving only the one child
[*Od.* VII.65]

6-1-3   had; I have taken away the mist from your eyes, that before
now [*Il.* V.127]

6-1-4   with fat, can then attempt to bend it, and finish the contest.'
[*Od.* XXI.180]

6-1-5   And now I see that of all my men it was only you two
[*Od.* XXI.209]

6-1-6   I will give him a mantle and tunic to wear, fine clothing, : I
will give him beautiful clothing to wear, a tunic and mantle.' :
I will give him fine clothing to wear, a mantle and tunic,
[*Od.* XVI.79; XVII.550; XXI.339]

6-2-1   knotting a noose and hanging sheer from the high ceiling,
[*Od.* XI.278]

6-2-2   remembering our excellence and what Zeus has established
[*Od.* VIII.244]

6-2-3   the great open water, since this is the gift of the Earthshaker
[*Od.* VII.35]

6-2-4   'Keep on with the bow, old fellow. You cannot do what
everyone [*Od.* XXI.369]

6-2-5   Rise up, then, to the fight and rouse the rest of the people.
[*Il.* XIX.139]

6-2-6   For not even the strength of Herakles fled away from
destruction, [*Il.* XVIII.117]

6-3-1   I am willing to make all good, and give back gifts in abundance.
: I am willing to make all good and give back gifts in abundance.
[*Il.* IX.120; XIX.138]

6-3-2   And let him stand up before the Argives and swear an oath to
you [*Il.* XIX.175]

6-3-3   "That man is here, we shall not look far for him, if you are willing [*Il.* XIV.110]

6-3-4   if he were to come suddenly, so, with the god leading him? [*Od.* XXI.196]

6-3-5   "All these things have been brought to fulfillment, nor in any other [*Il.* XIV.53]

6-3-6   Come on with me then. This work is better if many do it." [*Il.* XII.412]

6-4-1   it is the very gods who ruined the brain within you. : it is the very gods who ruined the brain within you, [*Il.* VII.360; XII.234]

6-4-2   "Do not fear, and let no thought of death be upon you. [*Il.* X.383]

6-4-3   mourning wake out of sleep her household's beloved companions, [*Il.* V.413]

6-4-4   But go on in silence while I lead the way for you, and do not [*Od.* VII.30]

6-4-5   still to reality, but your mind is gone and your discipline. [*Il.* XV.129]

6-4-6   to his son; but a son who never grew old in his father's armor. [*Il.* XVII.197]

6-5-1   is to go back to my house and see my day of homecoming. : grant me to reach my house and see my day of homecoming. [*Od.* V.220; VIII.466]

6-5-2   but Apollo of the silver bow then struck down Rhexenor, [*Od.* VII.64]

6-5-3   then there is hope that you can see your own people, and come back [*Od.* VII.76]

6-5-4   Therefore I will tell you the truth, and so it shall be; [*Od.* XXI.212]

6-5-5   And this also will I tell you and it will be a thing accomplished. [*Il.* I.212]

6-5-6   and send him wherever his heart and spirit desire to be sent. : and send him wherever his heart and spirit desire to be sent.' [*Od.* XVI.81; XXI.342]

6-6-1 swineherd? Those swift dogs that you raised yourself will feed on you [*Od.* XXI.363]

6-6-2 your saying; then you would see what kind of strength my hands have.' : then you yourself would see what kind of strength my hands have.' [*Od.* XX.237; XXI.202]

6-6-3 we do not think he will take you away. That is not likely. [*Od.* XXI.322]

6-6-4 keep on gathering here, all our days in expectation. [*Od.* XXI.156]

6-6-5 secret things and decide upon them. Never have you patience [*Il.* I.542]

6-6-6 "Do not, Dolon, have in your mind any thought of escape [*Il.* X.447]

DAYS AND HOURS FOR DIVINATION

The following lines are from *PGM* VII.155–67.[3]

at dawn	do not use
at noon	do not use
do not use	at dawn and in the afternoon
at dawn	at dawn
at dawn	at dawn
do not use	in the afternoon
at noon	in the afternoon
throughout the whole day	at dawn
do not use	at dawn
throughout the whole day	do not use
in the afternoon	in the afternoon
throughout the [whole] day	throughout the whole day
throughout the whole day	throughout the whole day
at dawn	throughout the whole day
throughout the whole day	in the afternoon

NOTES

INTRODUCTION

1. Majercik, *The Chaldæan Oracles,* 1.
2. Edmonds, *Drawing Down the Moon,* 343.
3. McCalla, "Illuminism and French Romantic Philosophies of History," 253–68.
4. Meyer, *The Nag Hammadi Scriptures,* 409–18.
5. Addey, *Divination and Theurgy in Neoplatonism,* 128.
6. Dodds, *The Greeks and the Irrational,* 140–41.
7. Lombardo, *Parmenides and Empedocles,* vii–viii.
8. Kingsley, *Ancient Philosophy, Mystery and Magic,* 303–4.
9. Naydler, "Plato, Shamanism and Ancient Egypt," 67–92.
10. Majercik, *The Chaldæan Oracles,* 193.
11. Inwood, *The Poem of Empedocles,* 265.
12. Lucid and Pontiac, *The Magic of the Orphic Hymns,* 266.
13. Lebedev, "The Aegean Origin and Early History of the Greek Doctrines," 240–301.
14. Kingsley, *A Story Waiting to Pierce You,* 4–6.
15. Cooper, *Plato: Complete Works,* 644.
16. Fontainelle, "The Greek *Iatromanteis.*"
17. Polosmak, "A Mummy Unearthed from the Pastures of Heaven," 80–103.
18. Fontainelle, "The Greek *Iatromanteis.*"
19. Fripp, "K. Crimson's Fripp: 'Music's Just a Means for Magic.'"
20. Lamberton, *Homer the Theologian,* 22–23.
21. Lamberton, 26.
22. Lamberton, 37.

23. Skinner, *Techniques of Graeco-Egyptian Magic,* 232.

24. Skinner, 232.

25. Stratton-Kent, *Geosophia: The Argo of Magic,* 141.

26. Betz, *The Greek Magical Papyri in Translation,* 112–18.

27. Kirk, "Homer."

28. Mackenzie, *Poetry and Poetics in the Presocratic Philosophers,* 3.

29. Uždavinys, *The Heart of Plotinus,* 228.

30. Lamberton, *Homer the Theologian,* 22.

31. Too, *The Idea of the Library in the Ancient World,* 86.

I. *KATABASIS* AND THE PRESOCRATICS

1. Addey, *Divination and Theurgy in Neoplatonism,* 156–57.

2. Fortier, "The Far-Wanderer: Proclus on the Transmigration of the Soul," 305–25.

3. Cooper, *Plato: Complete Works,* 836.

4. Cooper, 93.

5. Cooper, 97.

6. Uždavinys, *Ascent to Heaven in Islamic and Jewish Mysticism,* 49–50.

7. Guthrie, *The Pythagorean Sourcebook and Library,* 63.

8. Guthrie, 58.

9. Guthrie, 58–59.

10. Guthrie, 64.

11. Kingsley, *In the Dark Places of Wisdom,* 53.

12. Parmenides, *Fragments,* 24–25.

13. Mourelatos, *The Route of Parmenides,* 42–43.

14. Kingsley, *In the Dark Places of Wisdom,* 115.

15. Inwood, *The Poem of Empedocles,* 219.

16. Johnston, *Hekate Soteira,* 150.

17. Edwards, "The Running Maiden from Eleusis and the Early Classical Image of Hekate."

18. Rinella, *Pharmakon,* 154.

19. Edmonds, *Drawing Down the Moon,* 14.

20. Collins, *Magic in the Ancient Greek World,* 60.

21. Ruck, *The Apples of Apollo,* 171.

22. Kingsley, *Catafalque,* 235.

23. Inwood, *The Poem of Empedocles,* 219.

24. Faraone, "Empedocles the Sorcerer and His Hexametrical *Pharmaka,*" 14–32.

25. Mackenzie, *Poetry and Poetics in the Presocratic Philosophers,* 1.

26. Graham, *The Texts of Early Greek Philosophy,* 101.

27. Ruck, *Sacred Mushrooms of the Goddess and the Secrets of Eleusis,* 94–95.

28. Ruck, *The Road to Eleusis,* 51–52.

29. Lewy, *Chaldæan Oracles and Theurgy,* 205–11.

30. Lattimore, *The Iliad of Homer,* 478.

31. Tanaseaunu-Döbler, *Theurgy in Late Antiquity,* 207.

32. Cooper, *Plato: Complete Works,* 1245.

33. Majercik, *The Chaldæan Oracles,* 69.

34. Copenhaver, *Hermetica,* 15.

35. Linden, *The Alchemy Reader,* 51.

36. Condos, *Star Myths of the Greeks and Romans,* 119–23.

37. d'Este and Rankine, *Hekate: Liminal Rites,* 103.

38. Betz, *The Greek Magical Papyri in Translation,* 497.

39. Betz, "Fragments from a Catabasis Ritual in a Greek Magical Papyrus," 287–95.

40. Betz, *The Greek Magical Papyri in Translation,* 80.

41. Johnston, *Restless Dead,* 238–42.

42. Hesiod, *Works and Days, Theogony and the Shield of Heracles,* 47.

43. Marzahn, *Babylon und das Neujahrsfest,* 29–30.

44. Kingsley, *In the Dark Places of Wisdom,* 53–54.

45. Kingsley, 53.

46. Uždavinys, *Orpheus and the Roots of Platonism,* 59.

47. Uždavinys, 62.

48. Kingsley, *Ancient Philosophy, Mystery and Magic,* 204.

49. Kingsley, 256.

50. Janko, "Forgetfulness in the Golden Tablets of Memory," 89–100.

51. Betz, *The Greek Magical Papyri in Translation,* 49.

2. PLATONIC ALLEGORIES AND MYTHS

1. Petty, *Fragments of Numenius of Apamea,* 41.

2. Westerink, *Anonymous Prolegomena to Platonic Philosophy,* 44.

3. Westerink, xxxviii.

4. Westerink, 48.

5. Westerink, xl.

6. Westerink, xxxvii.

7. Lamberton, *Homer the Theologian,* 175.

8. Cooper, *Plato: Complete Works,* 1132–33.

9. Cooper, 1133–34.

10. Cooper, 1134.

11. Lamberton, *Homer the Theologian,* 27–28.

12. Cooper, *Plato: Complete Works,* 1218.

13. Cooper, 1219–20.

14. Cooper, 1219.

15. Latura Beke, *Visible Gates in the Pagan Skies,* 45.

16. Goold, *Manilius: Astronomica,* 61–63.

17. Latura Beke, *Visible Gates in the Pagan Skies,* 47.

18. Cooper, *Plato: Complete Works,* 1239.

19. Cooper, 1240.

20. Latura Beke, *Visible Gates in the Pagan Skies,* 51.

21. Latura Beke, 51.

22. Fontainelle, "Episode 76: The *Chaldæan Oracles* and Theurgy."

23. Cooper, *Plato: Complete Works,* 1241.

24. Cooper, 1245.

25. Edmonds, *Drawing Down the Moon,* 329.

26. Cooper, *Plato: Complete Works,* 522–23.

27. Cooper, 542.

28. Chlup, *Proclus: An Introduction,* 175.

29. Chlup, 176.

30. Eiss, *Divine Madness,* 372–74.

31. Murchú, *The God Who Becomes Redundant,* 142.

32. Cooper, *Plato: Complete Works,* 524.

33. Müller, *The Upanishads,* 12–13.

34. Cooper, *Plato: Complete Works,* 525.

35. Cooper, 526.

36. Cooper, 585–86.

37. Uždavinys, *Philosophy and Theurgy in Late Antiquity,* 13.

38. Uždavinys, 13.

39. Cooper, *Plato: Complete Works,* 486.

40. Cooper, 29.

41. Cooper, 492–94.

42. Iamblichus, *On the Mysteries,* 65.

43. Dillon, *The Middle Platonists,* 384–96.

3. THE *CHALDÆAN ORACLES* AND THEURGY

1. Cooper, *Plato: Complete Works,* 1240.

2. Shaw, *Theurgy and the Soud,* 193.

3. Tanaseaunu-Döbler, *Theurgy in Late Antiquity,* 246.

4. Majercik, *The Chaldæan Oracles,* 2.

5. Lewy, *Chaldæan Oracles and Theurgy,* 252.

6. Cooper, *Plato: Complete Works,* 21.

7. Suda On Line: Byzantine Lexicography, s.v. "Ioulinaos."

8. Majercik, *The Chaldæan Oracles,* 2.

9. Majercik, 6.

10. Majercik, 6.

11. Finamore and Johnston, "The Chaldaean Oracles," 161–73.

12. Crowley, *Magick: Liber ABA,* 569.

13. Majercik, *The Chaldæan Oracles,* 9.

14. Finamore and Johnston, "The Chaldaean Oracles," 161–73.

15. Majercik, *The Chaldæan Oracles,* 9.

16. Nelson, "A Greek Votive Iynx-Wheel in Boston," 443–56.

17. Majercik, *The Chaldæan Oracles,* 10–11.

18. Majercik, 11–12.

19. Majercik, 105.

20. Johnston, "Rising to the Occasion," 165–94.

21. Tanaseaunu-Döbler, *Theurgy in Late Antiquity,* 28.

22. Thumiger, *The Life and Health of the Mind in Classical Greek Medical Thought,* 318.

23. Seng, "Demons and Angels in the Chaldaean Oracles," 46–85.

24. Majercik, *The Chaldæan Oracles,* 101.

25. Majercik, 137.

26. Majercik, 99.

27. Majercik, 99.

28. Majercik, 49.

29. Majercik, 47.

30. Chlup, *Proclus: An Introduction,* 178–79.

31. Chlup, 180.

32. Majercik, *The Chaldæan Oracles,* 91.

33. Majercik, 93.

34. Betz, *The Greek Magical Papyri in Translation,* 48.

35. Mazur, "The 'So-called Pipe' in the Mithras Liturgy, *PGM* IV.549."

36. Faivre, *Access to Western Esotericism,* 14–15.

37. Marx, *Sosipatra of Pergamum,* 36.

38. Dillon, "Plotinus and the Chaldaean Oracles," 131–40.

4. PLOTINUS AND THE PLATONIZING SETHIAN GNOSTICS

1. Mazur, *The Platonizing Sethian Background of Plotinus's Mysticism,* 11.

2. Plotinus, *The Enneads,* 206.

3. Plotinus, 29.

4. Mazur, *The Platonizing Sethian Background of Plotinus's Mysticism,* 139.

5. Meyer, *The Nag Hammadi Scriptures,* 537.

6. Pearson, "Theurgic Tendencies in Gnosticism," 253–57.

7. Shaw, *Theurgy and the Soul,* 210.

8. Addey, *Divination and Theurgy in Neoplatonism,* 201–5.

9. Chlup, *Proclus: An Introduction,* 177.

10. Chlup, 180.

11. Plotinus, *The Enneads,* 26.

12. Plotinus, 35.

13. Plotinus, 627.

14. Uždavinys, *Philosophy as a Rite of Rebirth,* 78.

15. Plotinus, *The Enneads,* 101.

16. Mazur, *The Platonizing Sethian Background of Plotinus's Mysticism,* 69–71.

17. Mazur, 28–29.

18. Mazur, 29–31.

19. Mazur, 32–34.

20. Mazur, 38.

21. Mazur, 41.

22. Mazur, 47–48.

23. Plotinus, *The Enneads,* 399.

24. Plotinus, 34–35.

5. HERMETICA AND THEURGY

1. Betz, *The Greek Magical Papyri in Translation*, 81.
2. Betz, 104.
3. Shaw, "Taking the Shape of the Gods," 136–69.
4. Johnston, "Animating Statues: A Case Study in Ritual," 445–77.
5. Iamblichus, *On the Mysteries*, 5.
6. Copenhaver, *Hermetica: The Greek* Corpus Hermeticum *and the Latin* Asclepius, 5–6.
7. Hanegraaff, *Hermetic Spirituality and the Historic Imagination*, 183–84.
8. Mazur, *The Platonizing Sethian Background of Plotinus's Mysticism*, 28–29.
9. Meyer, *The Nag Hammadi Scriptures*, 410.
10. Copenhaver, *Hermetica: The Greek* Corpus Hermeticum *and the Latin* Asclepius, 25.
11. Copenhaver, 15.
12. Meyer, *The Nag Hammadi Scriptures*, 415–16.
13. Bull, "Monkey Business," 75–94.
14. Hanegraaff, *Hermetic Spirituality and the Historic Imagination*, 292–93.
15. Bull, "Monkey Business," 75–94.
16. Hanegraaff, *Hermetic Spirituality and the Historic Imagination*, 290.
17. DeConick, "The Road for the Soul Is through the Planets," 37–74.
18. Copenhaver, *Hermetica: The Greek* Corpus Hermeticum *and the Latin* Asclepius, 80–81.
19. Copenhaver, 89–90.

PART II.
THE *ODYSSEY* AND THE *ILIAD*

1. Lattimore, *The Odyssey of Homer*, 201.
2. Lattimore, *The Iliad of Homer*, 477–78.

6. PORPHYRY'S *ON THE CAVE OF THE NYMPHS*

1. Addey, *Divination and Theurgy in Neoplatonism*, 288.
2. Addey, 288.
3. Addey, 288.
4. Addey, 288.

5. Addey, 288.

6. Addey, 168.

7. Fontainelle, " Episode 129: Nilüfer Akçay on Porphyry's *On the Cave of the Nymphs*."

8. Uždavinys, *Philosophy as a Rite of Rebirth*, 78.

9. Uždavinys, *Philosophy and Theurgy in Late Antiquity*, 132.

10. Uždavinys, *The Heart of Plotinus*, 224.

11. Hill, *Concordia: The Roots of European Thought*, 74–77.

12. Burckhardt, *Mirror of the Intellect*, 162.

13. Uždavinys, *Philosophy As a Rite of Rebirth*, 279.

14. Lamberton, *Homer the Theologian*, 40.

15. Lamberton, *Homer the Theologian*, 41.

16. Lamberton, 115–17.

17. Lamberton, 225.

18. Lamberton, 226.

19. Lamberton, 42.

20. Uždavinys, *Philosophy as a Rite of Rebirth*, 279.

21. Stratton-Kent, *Geosophia*, 141–45.

22. Lattimore, *The Odyssey of Homer*, 169.

23. Uždavinys, *The Heart of Plotinus*, 252.

24. Stratton-Kent, *Geosophia*, 141–45.

25. Lamberton, *Homer the Theologian*, 53.

26. Uždavinys, *Philosophy as a Rite of Rebirth*, 280.

27. Petty, *Fragments of Numenius of Apamea*, 73.

28. Uždavinys, *Philosophy as a Rite of Rebirth*, 280.

29. Lamberton, *Homer the Theologian*, 41.

30. Lamberton, 113.

31. Dillon, *The Middle Platonists*, 236.

32. Uždavinys, *The Heart of Plotinus*, 236.

33. Dillon, *The Middle Platonists*, 363.

34. Petty, *Fragments of Numenius of Apamea*, 75.

35. Petty, 97.

36. Majercik, *The Chaldæan Oracles*, 51.

37. Petty, *Fragments of Numenius of Apamea*, 29.

38. Lattimore, *The Odyssey of Homer*, 201.

39. Mihai, "Porfirio, Sullo Stige. Testo greco a fronte, 99."

40. Lamberton, *Homer the Theologian*, 113.

41. Lamberton, 125.

42. Uždavinys, *The Heart of Plotinus,* 249.

43. Uždavinys, 250–52.

44. Uždavinys, 253–63.

45. Uždavinys, 253–63.

46. Petty, *Fragments of Numenius of Apamea,* 73.

47. Lattimore, *The Odyssey of Homer,* 345.

48. Uždavinys, *The Heart of Plotinus,* 255.

49. Latura Beke, *Visible Gates in the Pagan Skies,* 7–9.

50. Latura Beke, 9.

51. Stahl, *Commentary on the Dream of Scipio by Macrobius,* 135.

52. Stahl, 135.

53. Stahl, 135.

54. Stahl, 135.

55. Lattimore, *The Odyssey of Homer,* 201.

56. Uždavinys, *The Heart of Plotinus,* 255.

57. DeConick, "The Road for the Soul Is through the Planets," 37–74.

58. DeConick, 37–74.

59. Schmemann, *Of Water and the Spirit,* 75–80.

60. DeConick, "The Road for the Soul Is through the Planets," 37–74.

61. DeConick, 37–74.

62. Hatsis, *The Witches' Ointment,* 78–96.

63. Fatur, "Sagas of the Solanaceae."

64. U.S. Forest Service, "The Powerful Solanaceae: Henbane."

65. Muraresku, *The Immortality Key,* 118–19.

66. Hanegraaff, "Enter: The Gods (Interview)."

67. DeConick, "The Road for the Soul Is through the Planets," 37–74.

68. DeConick, 37–74.

69. DeConick, 37–74.

70. DeConick, 37–74.

71. DeConick, 37–74.

72. DeConick, 37–74.

73. DeConick, 37–74.

74. Evans, "Ritual in the *Second Book of Jeu,*" 137–59.

75. Frisvold, *Palo Mayombe: The Garden of Blood and Bones,* 59.

76. DeConick, "The Road for the Soul Is through the Planets," 37–74.

77. DeConick, 37–74.

78. DeConick, 37–74.

79. DeConick, 37–74.

80. Uždavinys, *The Heart of Plotinus,* 253–63.

81. Uždavinys, 253–63.

82. Richmond, *The Odyssey of Homer,* 345.

83. Lattimore, 296–97.

84. Anghelina, "The Homeric Gates of Horn and Ivory," 65–72.

85. Latura Beke, *Visible Gates in the Pagan Skies,* 13–15.

86. Latura Beke, 17.

87. Latura Beke, 19.

88. Latura Beke, 19.

7. PROCLUS'S *COMMENTARY ON PLATO'S REPUBLIC*

1. Proclus, *The Philosophical and Mathematical Commentaries of Proclus,* 32.

2. D'Hoine, *All from One: A Guide to Proclus,* 6.

3. Lamberton, *Homer the Theologian,* 16.

4. Lamberton, 17.

5. Graham, *The Texts of Early Greek Philosophy,* 109.

6. Lamberton, *Homer the Theologian,* 21–22.

7. Lamberton, 16.

8. Chlup, *Proclus: An Introduction,* 186–87.

9. Chlup, 190.

10. Chlup, 191.

11. Lamberton, *Homer the Theologian,* 199–200.

12. Lattimore, *The Iliad of Homer,* 477.

13. Cooper, *Plato: Complete Works,* 1029.

14. Proclus, *Commentary on Plato's Republic Vol. I: Essays 1–6,* 265.

15. Proclus, 265.

16. Proclus, 174.

17. Proclus, 265.

18. Uždavinys, "Putting on the Form of the Gods."

19. Shaw, *Theurgy and the Soul,* 130.

20. Lattimore, *The Iliad of Homer,* 476.

21. Uždavinys, *Philosophy and Theurgy in Late Antiquity,* 217.

22. Uždavinys, 159.

23. Lewy, *Chaldæan Oracles and Theurgy,* 205–6.

24. Majercik, *The Chaldæan Oracles,* 37–38.

25. Proclus, *Commentary on Plato's Republic,* 266.

26. Plotinus, *The Enneads,* 258.

27. Uždavinys, "Putting on the Form of the Gods."

28. Finamore, "Proclus on Ritual Practice in Neoplatonic Religious Philosophy," 121–38.

29. Lucid and Pontiac, *The Magic of the Orphic Hymns,* 266.

30. Lucid and Pontiac, 267.

31. Proclus, *Commentary on Plato's Republic,* 266.

32. Uždavinys, *The Heart of Plotinus,* 250.

33. Lattimore, *The Odyssey of Homer,* 201.

34. Uždavinys, *The Heart of Plotinus,* 252.

35. Uždavinys, 250.

36. Uždavinys, 251.

37. Uždavinys, 252.

38. Uždavinys, 255.

39. Lattimore, *The Iliad of Homer,* 478.

40. Lattimore, 474.

41. Proclus, *Commentary on Plato's Republic,* 266–67.

42. Finamore, "Proclus on Ritual Practice in Neoplatonic Religious Philosophy," 121–38.

43. Proclus, *Commentary on Plato's Republic,* 267.

44. Finamore, "Proclus on Ritual Practice in Neoplatonic Religious Philosophy," 121–38.

45. Finamore, "Proclus on Ritual Practice in Neoplatonic Religious Philosophy," 121–38.

46. Lattimore, *The Iliad of Homer,* 478.

47. Cooley, "Inana and Šukaletuda: A Sumerian Astral Myth," 161–72.

48. Proclus, *Commentary on Plato's Republic,* 267.

49. Edmonds, *Drawing Down the Moon,* 343.

8. ANIMATED *AGALMATA*

1. Uždavinys, *Philosophy and Theurgy in Late Antiquity,* 123.

2. Uždavinys, *Philosophy as a Rite of Rebirth,* 227.

3. Lattimore, *The Iliad of Homer,* 406–7.

4. Morris, *Daidalos and the Origins of Greek Art,* 11.

5. Morris, 11.

6. Cooper, *Plato: Complete Works,* 1338.

7. Naydler, *Temple of the Cosmos.*

8. Chlup, *Proclus: An Introduction,* 167.

9. Uždavinys, *Philosophy and Theurgy in Late Antiquity,* 65.

10. Tanaseaunu-Döbler, *Theurgy in Late Antiquity,* 228.

11. Tanaseaunu-Döbler, 155.

12. Uždavinys, *Philosophy and Theurgy in Late Antiquity,* 172–73.

13. Uždavinys, 173.

14. Plotinus, *The Enneads,* 399.

15. Edmonds, *Drawing Down the Moon,* 333.

16. Majercik, *The Chaldæan Oracles,* 91.

17. Chlup, *Proclus: An Introduction,* 170.

18. Faivre, *Western Esotericism: A Concise History,* 12.

19. Edmonds, *Drawing Down the Moon,* 334.

20. Edmonds, 334.

21. Iamblichus, *On the Mysteries,* 269.

22. Frisvold, *Palo Mayombe: The Garden of Blood and Bones,* 13.

23. Frisvold, 48.

24. Achad, *Q.B.L. or the Bride's Reception,* xiii.

25. Hanegraaff, *Hermetic Spirituality and the Historic Imagination,* 327.

26. Iamblichus, *On the Mysteries,* 115.

27. Chlup, *Proclus: An Introduction,* 90.

28. Majercik, *The Chaldæan Oracles,* 137.

29. Bostock, "Pliny the Elder, Natural History."

30. Bostock.

31. Dodoens, "Van Ruyte. Cap. lxix."

32. Çelik, "An Ethnobotanical Study in Pöhrenk Village," 131–41.

33. Ciaraldi, "Drug Preparation in Evidence?," 91–98.

34. Wedeck, *Love Potions through the Ages,* 221.

35. Ochoa, *Society of the Dead: Quita Manaquita and Palo Praise in Cuba,* 197.

36. Bhad et al., "The Lizard: An Unconventional Psychoactive Substance," 113–14.

37. Garg et al., "Addiction to Lizard: A Rare Case Report," 206.

38. Bostock, "Pliny the Elder, Natural History."

39. Tishma, "More Than 'Toil and Trouble': Macbeth and Medicine."

40. Tishma.

41. Dzwiza, "Daily Ancient Magic #9."

42. Woodruff, "7 Mind-Expanding Facts about Psychedelic History."

43. Voogelbreinder, *Garden of Eden,* 359.

44. Voogelbreinder, 262.

45. Nemu, "Getting High with the Most High."

46. Nemu.

47. Ferber et al., "The 'Entourage Effect'," 87–96.

48. Bourgeois et al., "Taking the Spice Routes," 21–32.

49. Nemu, "Getting High with the Most High."

50. Lattimore, *The Odyssey of Homer,* 70–71.

51. Lattimore, 139–40.

52. Lattimore, 155–67.

53. Lattimore, 159.

54. Hippolytus, *Refutation of All Heresies,* 155.

55. Uždavinys, *Philosophy and Theurgy in Late Antiquity,* 151.

56. Uždavinys, 159.

57. Uždavinys, 221.

CONCLUSION

1. Uždavinys, "Putting on the Form of the Gods."

APPENDIX: *HOMEROMANTEION*

1. Betz, *The Greek Magical Papyri in Translation,* 112–18.

2. Addey, *Divination and Theurgy in Neoplatonism,* 73.

3. Betz, *The Greek Magical Papyri in Translation,* 119.

BIBLIOGRAPHY

Achad, Frater. *Q.B.L. or the Bride's Reception*. Austin, Tex.: 100th Monkey Press, 2010.

Addey, Crystal. *Divination and Theurgy in Neoplatonism: Oracles of the Gods*. New York: Routledge, 2014.

Akçay, K. Nilüfer. *Porphyry's* On the Cave of the Nymphs *in its Intellectual Context*. Boston: Brill, 2019.

Anghelina, Catalin. "The Homeric Gates of Horn and Ivory." *Museum Helveticum* 67, no. 2 (2010): 65–72.

Anonymous. *Prolegomena to Platonic Philosophy*. Translated by L. G. Westerink. Gloucestershire, UK: Prometheus Trust, 2011.

Apuleius. *Metamorphoses,* Books 7–11. Edited and translated by J. Arthur Hanson. Cambridge, Mass.: Harvard University Press, 1989.

Betz, Hans Dieter. "Fragments from a Catabasis Ritual in a Greek Magical Papyrus." *History of Religions* 19, no. 4 (May, 1980): 287–95.

———. *The Greek Magical Papyri in Translation*. Chicago: University of Chicago Press, 1996.

Bhad, Roshan, Atul Ambekar, and Prabhoo Dayal. "The Lizard: An Unconventional Psychoactive Substance?" *Journal of Substance Use* 21, no. 2 (2016): 113–14.

Bostock, John. "Pliny the Elder, Natural History." Perseus Digital Library.

Bourgeois, James A., Usha Parthasarathi, and Ana Hategan "Taking the Spice Route: Psychoactive Properties of Culinary Spices." *Current Psychiatry* 13, no. 4 (April 2014): 21–32.

Bull, Christian. "Monkey Business: Magical Vowels and Cosmic Levels in the

Discourse on the Eighth and the Ninth" (NHC VI, 6). *Studi e materiali di Storia delle Religioni* 83, no. 1 (2017): 75–94.

Burckhardt, Titus. *Mirror of the Intellect: Essays on Traditional Science and Sacred Art.* Translated and edited by William Stoddart. Albany: State University of New York Press, 1987.

Çelik, Berfin. "An Ethnobotanical Study in Pöhrenk Village (Çiçekdağı-Kırşehir province / Turkey)." *Journal of Pharmacy of Istanbul University* 5, no. 2 (2000): 131–41.

Chlup, Radek. *Proclus: An Introduction.* Cambridge, UK: Cambridge University Press, 2012.

Ciaraldi, Marina. "Drug Preparation in Evidence? An Unusual Plant and Bone Assemblage from the Pompeian Countryside, Italy." *Vegetarian History and Archeobotany* 9 (2000): 91–98.

Collins, Derek. *Magic in the Ancient Greek World.* Malden, Mass.: Blackwell, 2008.

Condos, Theony. *Star Myths of the Greeks and Romans: A Sourcebook.* Grand Rapids, Mich.: Phanes Press, 1997.

Cooley, Jeffrey L. "Inana and Šukaletuda: A Sumerian Astral Myth." *Kaskal: A Journal of History, Environments, and Cultures of the Ancient Near East* 5 (2008): 161–72.

Cooper, John M. *Plato: Complete Works.* Indianapolis, Ind.: Hackett, 1997.

Copenhaver, Brian P. *Hermetica: The Greek* Corpus Hermeticum *and the Latin* Asclepius. Cambridge, UK: Cambridge University Press, 2000.

Crowley, Aleister. *Magick: Liber ABA.* San Francisco: Weiser Books, 2008.

DeConick, April D. "The Road for the Soul Is through the Planets." In *Practicing Gnosis: Ritual, Magic, Theurgy and Liturgy in Nag Hammadi, Manichean and Other Ancient Literature. Essays in Honor of Birger A. Pearson,* 37–74. Edited by April D. DeConick, Gregory Shaw, and John D. Turner. Boston: Brill, 2013.

d'Este, Sorita, and David Rankine. *Hekate: Liminal Rites.* London: Avalonia, 2009.

D'Hoine, Peter. *All from One: A Guide to Proclus.* New York: Oxford University Press, 2017.

Dillon, John. *The Middle Platonists.* Ithaca, N.Y.: Cornell University Press, 1996.

———. "Plotinus and the Chaldaean Oracles." In *Plato in Late Antiquity,* 131–40. Notre Dame, Ind.: University of Notre Dame Press, 1992.

Dodds, E. R. *The Greeks and the Irrational.* Berkeley: University of California Press, 1951.

Dodoens, Rembert. "Van Ruyte. Cap. Ixix." Chapter 69 in *Des Cruijdeboeck,* part 1, 128–31. Amsterdam, 1554. Plant Aardig Heden (website).

Dzwiza, Krista. "Daily Ancient Magic #9: Code Names for Ritual Ingredients." *Charaktêres: Ancient Magic and Ritual Practice Knowledge Hub* (blog). AWOL—The Ancient World Online.

Edmonds, Radcliffe G. *Drawing Down the Moon: Magic in the Greco-Roman World.* Princeton, N.J.: Princeton University Press, 2019.

Edwards, Charles M. "The Running Maiden from Eleusis and the Early Classical Image of Hekate." *American Journal of Archaeology* 90, no. 3 (1986): 307–18.

Eiss, Harry. *Divine Madness.* Newcastle upon Tyne, UK: Cambridge Scholars, 2011.

Eliade, Mircea. *Shamanism: Archaic Techniques of Ecstasy.* Princeton, N.J.: Princeton University Press, 2004.

Eusebius. *Preparation for the Gospel.* Translated by Edwin Hamilton Gifford. Eugene, Ore.: Wipf and Stock, 2002.

Evans, Erin. "Ritual in the *Second Book of Jeu.*" In *Practicing Gnosis: Ritual, Magic, Theurgy and Liturgy in Nag Hammadi, Manichean and Other Ancient Literature. Essays in Honor of Birger A. Pearson,* 137–59. Edited by April D. DeConick, Gregory Shaw, and John D. Turner. Boston: Brill, 2013.

Faivre, Antoine. *Access to Western Esotericism.* Albany: State University of New York Press, 1994.

———. *Western Esotericism: A Concise History.* Albany, N.Y.: SUNY Press, 2010.

Faraone, Christopher. "Empedocles the Sorcerer and His Hexametrical *Pharmaka.*" *Antichthon* 53 (2019): 14–32.

Fatur, Karsten. "Sagas of the Solanaceae: Speculative Ethnobotanical Perspectives on the Norse Berserkers." *Journal of Ethnopharmacology* 244 (November 15, 2019).

Ferber, Sari Goldstein, Dvora Namdar, Danielle Hen-Shoval, Gilad Eger, Hinanit Koltai, Gal Shoval, Liat Shbiro, and Aron Weller. "The 'Entourage Effect': Terpenes Coupled with Cannabinoids for the Treatment of Mood Disorders and Anxiety Disorders." *Current Neuropharmacology* 18, no. 2 (2020): 87–96.

Finamore, John F., and Sarah Iles Johnston. "The Chaldaean Oracles." In *The Cambridge History of Philosophy in Late Antiquity,* vol. 1., 161–73. Edited by Lloyd Gerson. Cambridge, UK: Cambridge University Press, 2016.

———."Proclus on Ritual Practice in Neoplatonic Religious Philosophy." In *Being or Good?: Metamorphoses of Neoplatonism,* edited by Agnieszka Kijewska, 121–38. Lublin, Poland: KUL, 2004.

Fontainelle, Earl. "Episode 76: The *Chaldæan Oracles* and Theurgy," November 27, 2019. *The Secret History of Western Esotericism Podcast.*

———. "The Greek *Iatromanteis*: *Katabasis*, Metempsychosis, Soul-Flight, and the Question of 'Shamanism,'" no date. *The Secret History of Western Esotericism Podcast.*

———. "Episode 129: Nilüfer Akçay on Porphyry's *On the Cave of the Nymphs,*" December 8, 2021. *The Secret History of Western Esotericism Podcast.*

Fortier, Simon. "The Far-Wanderer: Proclus on the Transmigration of the Soul." *Classical Quarterly* 68, no. 1 (2018): 305–25.

Fripp, Robert. "K. Crimson's Fripp: 'Music's Just a Means for Magic.'" Interview by Cameron Crowe. *Rolling Stone* 149, December 6, 1973. The Uncool.

Frisvold, Nicholaj de Mattos. *Palo Mayombe: The Garden of Blood and Bones.* London: Scarlet Imprint, 2010.

Garg, Mehak, Balwant S. Sidhu, and Rajnish Raj. "Addiction to Lizard: A Rare Case Report." *Indian Journal of Psychiatry* 56, no. 2 (April–June 2014): 206.

Goold, G. P. *Manilius: Astronomica.* Cambridge, Mass.: Harvard University Press, 2006.

Graham, Daniel W., trans. and ed. *The Texts of Early Greek Philosophy: The Complete Fragments and Selected Testimonies of the Major Presocratics,* Part I. Cambridge, UK: Cambridge University Press, 2014.

Guthrie, Kenneth Sylvan. *The Pythagorean Sourcebook and Library.* Grand Rapids, Mich.: Phanes Press, 1988.

Hanegraaff, Wouter. "Enter: The Gods (Interview)." Interview by Jena Nenadalove. *Legalicize,* 2020. *Creative Reading* (blog), posted September 25, 2020.

———. *Hermetic Spirituality and the Historic Imagination: Altered States of Knowledge in Late Antiquity.* Cambridge, UK: Cambridge University Press, 2022.

Hatsis, Thomas. *The Witches' Ointment: The Secret History of Psychedelic Magic.* Rochester, Vt.: Park Street Press, 2015.

Hesiod. *Theogony, Works and Days, Testimonia.* Edited and translated by Glenn W. Most. Cambridge, Mass.: Harvard University Press, 2018.

———. *Works and Days, Theogony and the Shield of Heracles.* Translated by Hugh G. Evelyn White. Mineola, N.Y.: Dover, 2006.

Hill, Stephen R. *Concordia: The Roots of European Thought*. London: Duckworth, 1992.

Hippolytus. *Refutation of All Heresies*. Translated by M. David Litwa. Atlanta, Ga.: SBL Press, 2016.

Iamblichus. *On the Mysteries*. Translated by Emma C. Clark. Atlanta, Ga.: SBL Press, 2003.

Inwood, Brian. *The Poem of Empedocles*. Toronto: University of Toronto Press, 2001.

Johnston, Sarah Iles. "Animating Statues: A Case Study in Ritual." In *Arethusa*, 445–77. Baltimore, Md.: Johns Hopkins University Press, 2008.

Johnston, Sarah Iles. *Hekate Soteira: A Study of Hekate's Roles in the Chaldean Oracles and Relates Literature*. Atlanta, Ga.: Scholars Press, 1990.

Johnston, Sarah Iles. *Restless Dead: Encounters between the Living and the Dead in Ancient Greece*. Berkeley: University of California Press, 1999.

———. "Rising to the Occasion: Theurgic Ascent in Its Cultural Milieu." In *Envisioning Magic,* 165–94. Edited by Peter Schäfer and Hans G. Kippenberg. New York: Brill, 1997.

Kingsley, Peter. *Ancient Philosophy, Mystery and Magic: Empedocles and Pythagorean Tradition*. Oxford, UK: Clarendon Press, 2009.

———. *Catafalque: Carl Jung and the End of Humanity*. London: Catafalque Press, 2018.

———. *In the Dark Places of Wisdom*. Point Reyes, Calif.: Golden Sufi Center, 2021.

———. *A Story Waiting to Pierce You: Mongolia, Tibet and the Destiny of the Western World*. Point Reyes, Calif.: Golden Sufi Center, 2018.

Kirk, Geoffrey S. "Homer." In *Encylopaedia Britannica Online.*

Lamberton, Robert. *Homer the Theologian: Neoplatonist Allegorical Reading and the Growth of the Epic Tradition*. Berkeley: University of California Press, 1986.

Lattimore, Richmond. *The Iliad of Homer*. Chicago: University of Chicago Press, 2011.

———. *The Odyssey of Homer*. New York: HarperCollins, 2007.

Latura Beke, George. *Visible Gates in the Pagan Skies*. Scotts Valley, Calif.: CreateSpace, 2009.

Lebedev, Andrei V. "The Aegean Origin and Early History of the Greek Doctrines of Reincarnation and Immortality of the Soul." In *Myth, Ritual, Literature,* 240–301. Edited by J. V. Ivanova and N. B. Bogdanovich. Moscow: HSE Publishing House, 2022.

Lewy, Hans. *Chaldæan Oracles and Theurgy*. Paris: Institut d'Études Augustiniennes, 2011.

Linden, Stanton J. *The Alchemy Reader*. Cambridge, UK: Cambridge University Press, 2003.

Lombardo, Stanley, trans. *Parmenides and Empedocles: The Fragments in Verse Translation*. Eugene, Ore.: Wipf and Stock, 1982.

Lucid, Tamra, and Ronnie Pontiac. *The Magic of the Orphic Hymns*. Rochester, Vt.: Innter Traditions International, 2023.

Mackenzie, Tom. *Poetry and Poetics in the Presocratic Philosophers*. Cambridge, UK: Cambridge University Press, 2021.

Majercik, Ruth, trans. *The Chaldæan Oracles*. Gloucestershire, UK: Prometheus Trust, 2013.

Marx, Heidi. *Sosipatra of Pergamum: Philosopher and Oracle*. New York: Oxford University Press, 2021.

Marzahn, Joachim. *Babylon und das Neujahrsfest*. Berlin: Vorderasiatiches Museum.

Mazur, Alexander J. *The Platonizing Sethian Background of Plotinus's Mysticism*. Boston: Brill, 2021.

———. "The 'So-called Pipe.' In the Mithras Liturgy, *PGM* IV.549." Unpublished, 2002.

McCalla, Arthur. "Illuminism and French Romantic Philosophies of History." In *Western Esoterism and the Science of Religion*, 253–68. Edited by A. Faivre and W. Hanegraaff. Leuven, Belgium: Peeters.

Meyer, Marvin. *The Nag Hammadi Scriptures*. New York: Harper Collins, 2009.

Mihai, Adrian. Review of *Porfirio, Sullo Stige. Testo greco a fronte, 99,* by Cristiano Castelletti. *Bryn Mawr Classical Review,* 2008.

Morris, Sarah. P. *Daidalos and the Origins of Greek Art*. Princeton, N.J.: Princeton University Press, 1995.

Mourelatos, Alexander P. D. *The Route of Parmenides*. New Haven, Conn.: Yale University Press, 1970.

Müller, Max. *The Upanishads, Part II*. Mineola, N.Y.: Dover, 1962.

Muraresku, Brian C. *The Immortality Key: The Secret History of the Religion with No Name*. New York: St. Martin's Press, 2020.

Murchú, Diarmuid Ó. *The God Who Becomes Redundant*. Cork, Ireland: Mercier Press, 1986.

Naydler, Jeremy. "Plato, Shamanism and Ancient Egypt." *Temenos Academy Review* 9 (2006): 67–92.

————. *Temple of the Cosmos: The Ancient Egyptian Experience of the Sacred.* Rochester, Vt.: Inner Traditions International, 1996.

Nelson, Grace, W. "A Greek Votive Iynx-Wheel in Boston." *American Journal of Archaeology* 44, no. 4 (October–December 1940): 443–56.

Nemu, Danny. "Getting High with the Most High: Entheogens in the Old Testament." *Journal of Psychedelic Studies* 3, no. 2 (2019): 117–32.

Ochoa, Todd Ramón. *Society of the Dead: Quita Manaquita and Palo Praise in Cuba.* Berkeley: University of California Press, 2010.

Palmer, John. *Parmenides and Presocratic Philosophy.* Oxford, UK: Oxford University Press, 2009.

Parmenides. *Fragments.* Translated by David Gallop. Toronto: University of Toronto Press, 2013.

Pearson, Birger A. "Theurgic Tendencies in Gnosticism and Iamblichus's Conception of Theurgy." In *Neoplatonism and Gnosticism,* 253–57. Edited by Richard T. Wallis and Jay Bregman. Albany: State University of New York Press, 1992.

Petty, Robert. *Fragments of Numenius of Apamea.* Gloucestershire, UK: Prometheus Trust, 2012.

Plotinus. *The Enneads.* Edited by Lloyd P. Gerson. Cambridge, UK: Cambridge University Press, 2019.

Polosmak, Natalia. "A Mummy Unearthed from the Pastures of Heaven." *National Geographic,* October 1994, 80–103.

Proclus. *Commentary on Plato's Republic Vol. 1: Essays 1–6.* Edited and translated by Dirk Baltzly, John F. Finamore, and Graeme Miles. Cambridge, UK: Cambridge University Press, 2018.

————. *The Philosophical and Mathematical Commentaries of Proclus, on the First Book of Euclid's Elements.* Translated by Thomas Taylor. London: T. Payne and Son, 1792.

Rinella, Michael. *Pharmakon: Plato, Drug Culture, and Identity in Athens.* Lanham, Md.: Lexington Books, 2012.

Ruck, Carl A. P. *The Apples of Apollo: Pagan and Christian Mysteries of the Eucharist.* Durham, N.C.: Carolina Academic Press, 2001.

————. *The Road to Eleusis: Unveiling the Secret of the Mysteries.* Berkeley, Calif.: North Atlantic Books, 2008.

————. *Sacred Mushrooms of the Goddess and the Secrets of Eleusis.* Berkeley, Calif.: Ronin, 2006.

Schmemann, Alexander. *Of Water and the Spirit: A Liturgical Study of Baptism.* Crestwood, N.Y.: St. Vladimir's Seminary Press, 1974.

Seng, Helmut. "Demons and Angels in the Chaldaean Oracles." In *Neoplatonic Demons and Angels,* 46–85. Edited by Luc Brisson, Seamus O'Neill, and Andrei Timotin. Boston: Brill, 2018.

Shaw, Gregory. "Taking the Shape of the Gods: A Theurgic Reading of Hermetic Rebirth." *Aries* 15 (2015): 136–69.

———. *Theurgy and the Soul: The Neoplatonism of Iamblichus.* Kettering, Ohio: Angelico Press/Sophia Perennis, 2014.

Skinner, Stephen. *Techniques of Graeco-Egyptian Magic.* Singapore: Golden Hoard Press, 2021.

Spiller, Henry, John R. Hale, and Jelle Z. De Boer. "The Delphic Oracle: A Multidisciplinary Defense of the Gaseous Vent Theory." *Journal of Toxicology. Clinical Toxicology* 40, no. 2 (February 2002): 189–96.

Stahl, William Harris. *Commentary on the Dream of Scipio by Macrobius.* New York: Columbia University Press., 1990.

Stratton-Kent, Jake. *Geosophia: The Argo of Magic,* Vol. 1. London: Scarlet Imprint, 2010.

Tanaseaunu-Döbler, Ilinca. *Theurgy in Late Antiquity: The Invention of a Ritual Tradition.* Göttingen, Germany: Vandenhoeck and Ruprecht, 2013.

Thumiger, Chiara. *The Life and Health of the Mind in Classical Greek Medical Thought.* Cambridge, UK: Cambridge University Press, 2017.

Tishma, Mariel. "More Than 'Toil and Trouble': Macbeth and Medicine." *Hekteon International: A Journal of Medical Humanities* 11, no. 4 (Fall 2019).

Too, Yun Lee. *The Idea of the Library in the Ancient World.* Oxford, UK: Oxford University Press, 2010.

U.S. Forest Service. "The Powerful Solanaceae: Henbane." U.S. Department of Agriculture.

Uždavinys, Algis. *Ascent to Heaven in Islamic and Jewish Mysticism.* London: Matheson Trust, 2011.

———. ed. *The Heart of Plotinus: The Essential Enneads.* Bloomington, Ind.: World Wisdom, 2009.

———. *Orpheus and the Roots of Platonism.* London: Matheson Trust, 2011.

———. *Philosophy and Theurgy in Late Antiquity.* Kettering, Ohio: Angelico Press/Sophia Perennis, 2014.

———. *Philosophy as a Rite of Rebirth: From Ancient Egypt to Neoplatonism.* Gloucestershire, UK: Prometheus Trust, 2008.

———. "Putting on the Form of the Gods: Sacramental Theurgy in Neoplatonism." *Sacred Web* 5 (2000): 107–20.

Voogelbreinder, Snu. *Garden of Eden: The Shamanic Use of Psychoactive Flora and Fauna, and the Study of Consciousness.* Victoria, Australia: Self-published, 2009.

Wedeck, Harry E. *Love Potions through the Ages: A Study of Amatory Devices and Mores.* New York: Citadel Press, 1963.

Westerink, L. G., trans. *Anonymous Prolegomena to Platonic Philosophy.* Gloucester, UK: Prometheus Trust, 2011.

Woodruff, Eden, and Tom Hatsis. "7 Mind-Expanding Facts About Psychedelic History." Psanctum Psychedelia, July 8, 2020.

INDEX